Remodelista in Maine

Also Available

Remodelista
Gardenista
Remodelista: The Organized Home

Remodelista in Maine

A DESIGN LOVER'S GUIDE TO INSPIRED, DOWN-TO-EARTH STYLE

ANNIE P. QUIGLEY
WITH THE EDITORS OF REMODELISTA
Photographs by Greta Rybus

ARTISAN | NEW YORK

Remodelista editor in chief Julie Carlson
Writer and producer Annie P. Quigley
Principal photographer Greta Rybus
DIY producer and photographer Justine Hand
Book designer Jennifer Wagner
Photo retoucher Sjoerd Langeveld
Illustrator Lucy Augé
Researchers Lily Edgerton, Eleanor McCole, Olivia Nash

Library of Congress Cataloging-in-Publication Data

Names: Quigley, Annie P., author. | Rybus, Greta, photographer (expression)
Title: Remodelista in Maine / Annie P. Quigley, with the editors of
   Remodelista ; photographs by Greta Rybus.
Description: New York : Artisan, a division of Workman Publishing Co., Inc. [2022] |
   Includes index.
Identifiers: LCCN 2021035099 | ISBN 9781648290152
Subjects: LCSH: Interior decoration—Maine. | Decoration and ornament—Maine.
Classification: LCC NK2002 .Q54 2022 | DDC 747.09741—dc23
LC record available at https://lccn.loc.gov/2021035099

Artisan books are available at special discounts when purchased in bulk for premiums and sales promotions as well as for fund-raising or educational use. Special editions or book excerpts also can be created to specification. For details, contact the Special Sales Director at the address below, or send an e-mail to specialmarkets@workman.com.

For speaking engagements, contact speakersbureau@workman.com.

Published by Artisan
A division of Workman Publishing Co., Inc.
225 Varick Street
New York, NY 10014-4381
artisanbooks.com

Artisan is a registered trademark of Workman Publishing Co., Inc.

Printed in China on responsibly sourced paper

First printing, April 2022

10 9 8 7 6 5 4 3 2 1

I would really rather feel bad in Maine
than feel good anywhere else.

—E. B. White

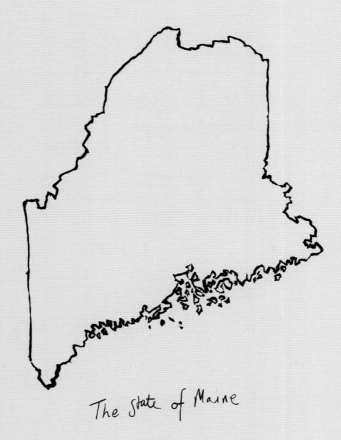

The state of Maine

Contents

Maine's design aesthetic is rooted in its ruggedness: its dark pine forests and rocky coast, the first place in the United States to be lit by sunrise each morning—this is, after all, the land of the Wabanaki, whose name means "People of the Dawn." Those who visit in summer know Maine for its beaches, seaside towns, and lobster shacks, but stay longer and you'll find there's a hardiness required to settle in and make a home here.

The Maine spirit is about rolling up your sleeves, using what you have, and reveling in nature, and it's evident in cottages and lakeside cabins, Portland town houses and rural farms. Our favorite Maine homes are lived-in, not decorated; equal parts practical and inspired; and wholly personal. Unchanged for generations or newly imagined, these spaces respect the land and tell the story of the people who inhabit them.

The last active Shaker village in the world is in Maine, and the Shaker ethos of beauty in simplicity runs through the objects and houses in this book. The state has long stirred artists and writers—from Winslow Homer to Edward Hopper, Edna St. Vincent Millay to Margaret Wise Brown—and a new generation of makers are coming here to continue the Maine tradition of slow, inspired living.

Mainers are also steadfast DIYers: If they need walls plastered or a wool blanket mended, they take it on themselves. This style can't be bought from a store—it comes from handed-down know-how, like how to slip warmed stones under the covers on cold winter nights, or stow a pair of clippers in the glove box for snipping roadside flowers. The Maine ways of creating a home are inherently eco-friendly, resourceful, and enduring.

This book is an homage to design Down East, featuring ten exceptional houses, from a hand-built dwelling in a clearing to an off-grid island home. There are also how-to guides from local shopkeepers, homesteaders, and chefs; our favorite Maine products (and where to get them); design-forward destinations to explore year-round; and simple seasonal projects to try yourself. Taken together, they serve as a pocket guide to bringing home a little bit of the Pine Tree State, no matter where you live.

Design Lessons from Maine

1. Do it yourself. Stacking wood? Repairing a leaky pipe? Cultivating a garden? The Maine spirit is about tackling tasks oneself. Putting elbow grease into your home, where possible, is more satisfying than hiring out.

2. A little sand never hurt anyone. The Maine houses we love are casual, never fussy, and designed for ease of living. Painted wood floors stand up to tracked-in beach sand. (A quick rinse of the feet from the hose before heading in helps, too.)

3. Look to the land. Think like a painter and draw from Maine's wild, untempered landscape for a color palette of quiet neutrals, deep blues, pine greens, even seaweed-esque ochre.

4. Natural is better than store-bought. Driftwood can be fashioned into a coat hook. Seaworn shells, branches, and fallen crab apples create soulful vignettes. A rock makes a great doorstop. Just remember to tread lightly and abide by the rules of parks and beaches before you begin foraging.

5. Every house should have a mudroom (and a good doormat). Mainers need a hardworking entryway for casting off muddy boots, stashing beach essentials, and storing a snow shovel and a pail of salt or sand for deicing the front steps. Even domiciles in less-wild climates benefit from an indoor/outdoor buffer zone, however small.

6. Think local. Maine runs on tight-knit communities. Bring back the sometimes-lost art of getting to know your neighbors: Shovel out the house next door after a snowstorm, borrow what you need, and lend what you can spare.

7. Stock up. Always be ready for a power outage (candles, flashlights, spare batteries, a wireless radio, pots filled with water), a winter storm (tinned food or—like in the old days—a root cellar), or a heat wave (fans, never AC; for more tips, see page 94).

8. Embrace all kinds of weather. Maine has four entirely different seasons (five, if you count mud season), and Mainers honor them in full. In summer, throw open the windows; rig up an ad hoc outdoor shower. In winter, bundle up and head outside for cross-country skiing, snowshoeing, or ice fishing—then warm up by the woodstove.

9. Layer. Mainers know the art of bundling up for frigid midwinter days and surprisingly cool summer nights—and the same can be said for their interior spaces. Add and subtract layers for the season: wool blankets in winter, easy cotton slipcovers in summer.

10. The view is the best decor. One thing we've seen time and again in Maine houses? The view out the window—whether garden or woods, lake or open ocean—is the art. Draw the eye toward the outside, frame with care, and keep everything else simple.

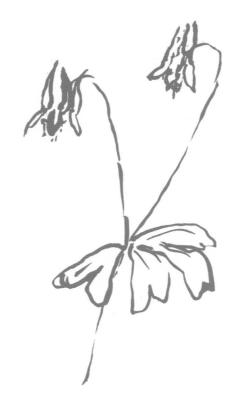

Columbine

Spring

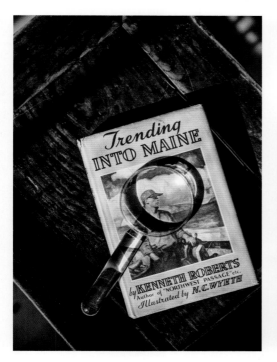

THE RESTORERS' HOUSE

A COUPLE REVIVED A SALTWATER
FARMHOUSE AND BARN—QUITE
LITERALLY DOWN TO THE HINGES.

When a pair of creatives found an 1840s farm on a rise above the Damariscotta River in South Bristol, they set aside their normally avant-garde style and turned instead toward recapturing the farmhouse's Early American spirit.

Together with architects Bruce Norelius and Zel Bowman-Laberge of Norelius Studio, based in Brooksville, Maine, and Santa Monica, California, the couple took their lead from the farmhouse's history and painstakingly restored the home with an elegant hand. Some changes (installing twenty-first-century electrical, plumbing, and heating systems, for example) were sweeping, others minute. The couple and the architects sourced the smallest of period details, sleuthing window latches, hinges, and hardware from vintage dealers and salvage shops. In peeling back walls, the team discovered a scrap of old wallpaper buried beneath the layers and hired James Randolph Rogers & Co. in England to reproduce it using a traditional woodblock printing method. The redone designs—in the original motif and in new palettes—now paper many of the rooms.

Out of doors, the couple embraced the ethos of the old farmstead, too, cultivating flower gardens, nurturing oysters in a small cove on the property, keeping bees ("though it's a challenge to overwinter them successfully in the Maine cold," the pair admits), even installing a traditional root cellar in the barn.

The house may be Early American in appearance, but it's fully modern beneath the surface, with solar panels added on the roof of the barn and Tesla batteries in the basement. Now, the homeowners say, they live through Maine's frequent power outages "without a hiccup."

1

1 Salvaged floors
The team replaced all the home's flooring, swapped out in the 1930s, with period-appropriate wide-plank boards. Here, the couple's "demanding but benevolent" Italian greyhound stands at attention by the front door.

2 Hardworking entry
A sunken mudroom is fitted with built-in storage bins and drawers.

4

3 Utility sink
The generously sized slate washbasin
was designed by Norelius Studio.
"It's great for preparing flowers for
arranging and for bathing the dog,"
the homeowners say.

4 Robin's-egg hue
A springy blue color carries through
the sunken entry, dining area, and
kitchen on trim and built-ins; it's the
fittingly named Cook's Blue from
Farrow & Ball.

5 Two-tone prep space
The countertops are a rustic-sophisticated mix of quartersawn white oak and marble.

6 Period-appropriate cladding
Shiplap and a beadboard ceiling help delineate the kitchen from the rest of the room.

7 Furniture in the kitchen
The cabinets have the look of individual cupboards, creating the feeling of an old-world scullery.

8 Overhead spotlights
P&S Alabax porcelain flush-mount lights from Rejuvenation illuminate the work space.

9 Farmhouse sink
A double-basin apron-front sink by English company Shaws provides copious space for dish-washing.

10 Simple storage
In lieu of upper cabinets, open corner shelves corral glassware and ceramics.

11 Classic Americana
The couple won the Rysdyk's Hambletonian horse painting at a local auction.

12 Old-fashioned larder
A built-in hutch offers extra storage for vintage cookware and mixing bowls.

11

12

13

14

15

16

13 A Maine classic
A shell makes a lovely (and no-cost) soap dish.

14 Tiny details, big impact
The unlacquered brass switch plates used throughout the home are from Kyle Switch Plates.

15 Modern amenity
The homeowners made only one tweak to the layout: adding an en suite bathroom to the main bedroom upstairs.

16 Brass is best
Among the architects' favorite sources for hardware are House of Antique Hardware, Nor'East Architectural Antiques, and Maine-based Casey's Wood Products. The team also commissioned local metalsmiths Erica Moody and Lowe Hardware to make custom brass TP holders and radiator fittings.

18

17 Twist on tradition
The couple flipped the traditional New England porch palette and painted the floors (not the ceilings) in St. Giles Blue from Farrow & Ball.

18 Old New England practicality
The antique barn was renovated to include a root cellar designed by Norelius and Canada-based expert Zach Loeks and built by Cold Mountain Builders. The couple uses it to preserve root vegetables and dahlia tubers over the winter.

19 Cutting garden
The couple worked with landscape architect Stephen Mohr and with Kevin O'Donnell of Sunset Knoll Landscaping to create a modern homestead of sorts, complete with prolific flower gardens.

19

21

20 Sowing seeds
A whimsically detailed greenhouse was added to the property "for seed starting, and for growing vegetables that appreciate more heat than Maine summers provide," the homeowners say.

21 Grown here
Raised vegetable beds, fenced to deter deer, yield fresh produce all spring and summer long.

How to Create Wild, Lush Flower Arrangements

ERIN FRENCH IS THE
SELF-TAUGHT CHEF BEHIND
THE LOST KITCHEN, A
RESTAURANT IN THE QUIET
TOWN OF FREEDOM THAT'S
BECOME PERHAPS THE MOST
IN-DEMAND RESERVATION IN
THE COUNTRY. EACH NIGHT
BEFORE SERVICE, SHE STEPS
AWAY FROM THE STOVE TO
ARRANGE LOCALLY GROWN
FLOWERS FOR EACH OF THE
TABLES. HERE ARE HER FIVE TIPS
FOR MAGICAL MAINE-INSPIRED
ARRANGEMENTS.

1 Winnow down. "Less is more.
Stick to flowers or a palette you
know you love."

2 Or follow the rule of odds.
"I've gotten into this thing of
doing three flowers, no more:
plentiful, but three different
kinds. Odd numbers look right
to the eye."

**3 Stash pruners in your
car.** Erin knows where to find
the best roadside blossoms:
elderflower, lupines, lilac. "When
I'm driving, I always keep my eyes
peeled for something awesome
I can forage. I store a saw in the
back of the car and pruners in
the glove box." (Just be careful
not to forage from private or

protected property—and to clip
in moderation.)

4 Buy vases for a song. No
need for fancy vessels—a simple
glass one will do. "I've never
spent more than twenty dollars
on a vase," Erin says. Inexpensive
versions can be found at IKEA; or
browse Etsy for vintage ones.

**5 Use slim branches as an
anchor.** Birch branches can
provide structure and stability for
large arrangements. Erin collects
them from the side of the road:
"That's what you do in Maine,"
she says.

Vinalhaven

THE ARCHITECTS' HOUSE

NESTLED ON A ROCKY
OUTCROPPING 90 FEET ABOVE
A COVE IS A MODERN TAKE ON
THE TRADITIONAL CONNECTED
FARMHOUSE, FILLED WITH
SURPRISING ECLECTICISM.

There's something old-fashioned about Maria Berman and Brad Horn's house on the island of Vinalhaven, fifteen miles from the mainland: the lines evoking a New England farmhouse, shingles weathering into the landscape. "We had been searching for a piece of land on which to build a house and found this property through friends," says Maria, who for years has been coming to Maine from New York City, where she and Brad run architecture firm Berman Horn Studio. "The land had never been built upon, but there are many stone walls from when this part of the island was pasture."

The architects designed a house split in two—a main house and a smaller guesthouse, a nod to the architecture of traditional farmhouses and barns in Maine. But theirs is a thoroughly streamlined version, clad in locally produced eastern white cedar shingles with no eaves or overhangs, and connected by a minimal addition: a pitched screened porch with a gridded aluminum frame. "This porch is really the beating heart of the house in summer, when living outside in Maine connects you even more closely to the surrounding land," Maria says. The landscape here feels untouched thanks to the couple's efforts to "minimize contractor creep" (trucks and supplies and machinery) on the upland heath throughout the building process. "We tried to simplify construction as much as possible and to use materials easily sourced from the island," says Maria.

Now it feels as though the wildness of the land just beyond the screens—juniper, lichens, grasses, scraggly spruces—is overtaking the house itself, spilling onto the simple wooden decks, even appearing inside, in moments of bright color and pattern and bunches of wildflowers. "The woods, sky, and ocean are filled with life," says Maria. "It's humbling and heartening to live among it."

1

1 Open-door policy
The wide peaked porch—the center of activity in warm weather—leads into the kitchen, dining area, and living space via two sets of double doors.

2 Sophisticated one-piece
The pared-back kitchen—made up of an island fitted with a cooktop, sink, storage, and a small fridge— keeps sight lines open and allows for gathering.

3

3 Unfussy floors
The floors are painted in hard-wearing deck paint by Benjamin Moore.

4 Fresh-air living
A bank of metal-framed windows offers views of the water (and echoes the lines of the porch).

5 Lofty ideas
A ladder to a sleeping loft and a cinder-block fireplace both emphasize the ceiling's height.

6 Simple forms
An all-white gabled interior is a
spare backdrop for colorful finds
and moments of eclecticism.

7 Architects' salvage
"The furniture is really from all
over," says Maria, citing flea markets,
antiques stores (like Marston House;
see page 122), estate sales, and even
the local Vinalhaven dump.

9

8 Indoor/outdoor living
"We envisioned the structure as slender and delicate, like a pencil line," says Maria of the porch. The couple wanted it to be lightweight and easily assembled, ideally "by one person on a standard ladder, with affordable and replaceable window screens."

9 Seeing green
The hues of a bedroom echo the meadows outside, with a deep green door and rocking chair, a quaint gingham headboard, and a colorful flat-weave rug.

10 Nods to nature
A Shaker box, a scrap of birch bark, and a vine-entwined nightstand make for a springy bedside vignette.

10

11

12

13

14

11 Easy catchalls
Woven baskets—tucked beneath a
bench and hung beside the door—
corral outdoor essentials in the
entryway.

12 Practical matters
A warm-weather Maine essential:
a flyswatter at the ready.

13 The slim guest room
A narrow bedroom is fitted with
two twin beds and a clever desk
Maria and Brad constructed out
of grayed cedar left over from the
deck construction. The cabinet was
salvaged from the Vinalhaven dump
swap shop.

14 Shifting light
"The house itself is like a sundial, with
the screened porch casting shadows
that fall differently throughout the day
and the seasons," says Maria. "We see
the sweep of the sun advance and
recede. Its movement is especially
powerful this far north."

15 A view from the shore
With these surroundings, the house needs no adornment. "Even on such a small island, we are constantly finding new places, beaches, trails, and other hidden wonders," says Maria.

How to Design a Plein Air Tablescape

MOLLY O'ROURKE IS THE VISIONARY DESIGNER BEHIND THE CAMDEN-BASED EVENT COMPANY ONE & SUPP, AND IN HER IMAGINATIVE, PLAYFUL TABLESCAPES, SHE'S JUST AS LIKELY TO USE MAINE POTATOES AS SCULPTURAL LOCAL CERAMICS. CREATIVITY RUNS IN THE FAMILY: MOLLY'S SISTER IS CLOTHING DESIGNER JULIE O'ROURKE (SEE PAGE 189), AND HER MOTHER IS THE PAINTER BEHIND SPRUCE TREE STUDIO (SEE PAGE 211). HERE, MOLLY SHARES HER SEVEN TIPS FOR SETTING A WHIMSICAL TABLE TO WELCOME THE RETURN OF WARM WEATHER AND LONGER DAYS—OR JUST BECAUSE.

1 Design around one focal point. "Perhaps you look out your window to see a perfect blushing branch of cherry blossoms," says Molly. One bough, placed in a simple glass vase, "can anchor a whole table. Love that gingham tablecloth? Build a picnic around it."

2 Let food double as decor. "An overflowing bowl of ripe summer fruits, branches of cherry tomatoes in a bud vase, or a wedge of cheese with torn bread can take center stage."

3 Enlist an apple corer. "It turns out an apple corer creates a hole that is the same diameter as a taper candle. Once I discovered this, there was no turning back. Use an apple corer to transform hunks of stale bread into improvised candlesticks. Potatoes, apples, cabbages, and melons all become sculptural candelabras that can be whipped up on the spot and composted after your event. The world is your candlestick."

4 Consider height and scale. Group similar objects together for an intriguing tableau. "When the eye moves along the table, it enjoys a visual feast—so many lovely little moments to take in."

CONTINUED

5 Create (artful) mash-ups.
"I find the best way to merge tabletop elements from different eras is to identify a common theme, color palette, or style," says Molly. "For this scene, I played with natural materials and colors to mimic the shapes and tones of the melons."

6 Dine by candlelight. "Keep a selection of tapers and votives"—preferably beeswax—"on hand, and light them at every meal."

7 Don't be afraid to play. "Design can be formal and rigorous, but it can also be playful and cheeky and forgiving. Have fun; try new things. Guests will feel your joy and creativity."

THE CURATOR'S HOUSE

AN ARTS DIRECTOR FOSTERS
COMMUNITY SPIRIT IN A
NINETEENTH-CENTURY CHURCH
TURNED LIVING QUARTERS (AND
SOMETIME PERFORMANCE SPACE).

This stately church in the town of Rockland would seem run-of-the-mill New England, except for one detail: "I painted it black," says homeowner Donna McNeil. "It was a shocker to many in the community, but there is a history of black churches in Iceland. At night, the large windows light up like enormous candles."

The church was built in 1851 by Hiram Berry, a master carpenter who would later become a Civil War general; by the time Donna, the executive director of a local arts foundation, found it in 2017, the major conversions to turn it into a home had been completed by the previous owner. But it was Donna who gave it its artfulness, painting the exterior in a shade of Rust-Oleum called Onyx and the interiors all white, and installing an uncommonly good-looking black IKEA kitchen. "I think better with clear surfaces and simple lines, but in my hedonist heart, I love a plethora of piled-up objects of beauty," says

Donna. With her artist's eye, vintage powder boxes, potted houseplants, even her trademark hats and boots become the display. "And of course," she adds, "plenty of art."

The vast sanctuary (the main living area is one 1,900-square-foot room; the tin ceilings are 21 feet high) is sometimes turned into a stage or a place for spontaneity. Donna occasionally invites young artists to stay with her; one resident organized "Bread, Soup, Cake" nights for the community; another, a cellist, offered a solo concert. "I've moved the furniture aside to host book readings and for planned and impromptu dance parties," says Donna; then, the white interiors become a life-size canvas for art of all kinds.

2

1 Arrangement as art object
Donna's approach to sourcing flowers and branches? "Thievery!" she jokes. "The flora come from nature. I don't buy anything."

2 Cost-conscious kitchen
Donna installed a clean-lined black-and-white kitchen on a budget, pairing IKEA cabinetry with Lowe's countertops. The black wall-mounted lights are "supercheap task lights from Amazon," says Donna; the standing light is the IKEA Hektar floor lamp.

3 Deconstructed living area
An Eero Saarinen Womb chair reupholstered in vintage Knoll fabric, a blue Danish chair, and an Italian Murano glass floor lamp from the 1950s create a sitting area in one corner of the sanctuary.

3

4 An extra dose of white
The floors are painted in three coats
of white oil-based enamel, adding to
the gallery-like effect.

5 Good bones
The main sanctuary is now the (very) open living space, with the altar and its filigree detailing at the far end.

6 Repurposed pews
A communal table is flanked by church pews that Donna found in the building and painted pitch black.

7 Flea-market finds
Among the vintage objects on display: alabaster lights from Antiques on Nine in Kennebunk.

8

9

10

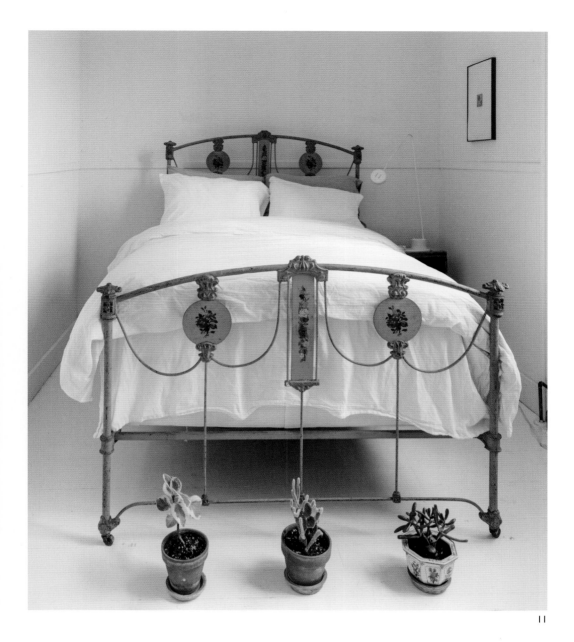

11

8 Marfa meets Maine
Donna made the daybed herself,
inspired by Donald Judd and a visit
to Marfa, Texas. The inside of an open
closet is painted a cheerful yellow.

9 Rule of three
A trio of vintage powder boxes is
displayed on a stair rail.

10 Spring green
The balcony leads to an all-white
bedroom—save for a green-painted
iron bed frame that Donna found
for seventy-five dollars on Craigslist.

11 Garden bed
A row of houseplants adds a bit of
whimsy to the foot of the bed.

13

14

12 Vintage pair
A Dutch door opens into one of four bedrooms, where Donna has hung a portrait of a friend's ancestor. "She is possibly of the same period as the house," Donna says. The chair came from an antiques shop in Fairfield, Maine.

13 Bed in a box
Donna's bedroom has a modern four-poster: "The silhouette mimics the shape of the space almost exactly, creating a room-in-a-room effect," she says.

14 Maine finds
A petite bathroom features a 1950s pastel portrait from a Camden antiques shop and a mirror found in Belfast. The Balinese mask was a gift from a friend.

Moses Eaton Stenciled Tea Towel

Before the industrial revolution made wallpaper more affordable, thrifty New Englanders employed folk artists like Moses Eaton and his eponymous son to stencil their bare walls with charming motifs. For a modern take on the Eatons' original designs, we've used their more graphic patterns (available from mbhistoricdecor.com) to create stenciled tea towels that are thoroughly of the moment.

MATERIALS

COTTON OR LINEN
TEA TOWEL, WASHED AND
IRONED

MASKING OR PAINTER'S TAPE

STENCIL ADHESIVE

MOSES EATON STENCIL

TEXTILE PAINT

SHALLOW DISH FOR PAINT

LARGE FLAT-TIPPED
PAINTBRUSH OR SPONGE

PAPER TOWEL

IRON

1 Lay a towel flat over a protected surface and secure the corners with tape. Make sure the fabric is taut. In a well-ventilated work space, spray the reverse side of your stencil with a light coat of adhesive, which will keep the stencil in place while you work and stop paint from running under it. Make sure you cover the whole surface, but do not oversaturate it, as the adhesive may stain the towel. Carefully lay the adhesive side of the stencil onto your towel, pressing around each edge.

2 Pour a small amount of paint into the shallow dish. Dip only the tip of the brush into the pigment and blot it onto a paper towel until the brush is almost dry. Holding the brush straight up and down, vigorously tap the fabric within the stencil pattern. Repeat, slowly building up thin layers of paint until you achieve a rich color.

3 Gently peel off the stencil. Allow the paint to dry thoroughly. Heat set with an iron according to the paint instructions, and wash the towel before use.

1

2

3

Pressed Seaweed Prints

Popularized in the nineteenth century, when the likes of John James Audubon inspired many budding naturalists, pressed seaweed makes a beguiling Maine keepsake. On beach walks, keep your eye out for washed-ashore examples worth preserving and displaying.

Pressed Seaweed Prints

MATERIALS

SEAWEED

2 TUBS, TRAYS, OR BAKING DISHES (ONE LARGE ENOUGH TO ACCOMMODATE YOUR PAPER)

WATERCOLOR OR OTHER THICK PAPER

CARDBOARD

BOARDS

PAINTBRUSH

WEED BARRIER LANDSCAPE FABRIC

STONES, BRICKS, BOOKS, OR OTHER ITEMS TO SERVE AS WEIGHTS

1 Collect an array of feathery seaweeds along the shore. Rinse the specimens in a tub filled with fresh water.

2 Fill a separate tub or tray with at least 1½ inches of fresh water and submerge a piece of watercolor paper. Arrange a seaweed specimen on top of the paper.

3 Tilting the paper so the water runs off, gently ease it out of the water and rest it on two pieces of cardboard. (To protect your working surface, we recommend placing a board beneath the first layer of cardboard.) Use a paintbrush to remove any debris.

4 Place a piece of landscape fabric over your work, followed by two more pieces of cardboard. Repeat, layering another piece of watercolor paper, another specimen, and two more pieces of cardboard, until you reach your desired number of prints. Finally, add a top board and weight it down with stones or whatever heavy objects you have on hand. Leave your pressings in a well-ventilated, dry spot. Check after two days and change the cardboard if it is too wet. Check again in a couple of days, changing the cardboard again, if necessary, until the specimens are dry.

NOTE: Label your pressed seaweed, if you wish, before hanging. Head to the Maine Seaweed Council (seaweedcouncil .org/identifying-maine-seaweeds) to ID your Down East finds, or find a website specific to the place where you live.

1

2

3

4

lupine

Summer

THE OFF-GRID HOUSE

A WRITER AND A RETIRED JUDGE BUILT A SHIPSHAPE HOUSE ON A REMOTE ISLAND, WITH RAINWATER COLLECTED FROM THE ROOF AND TENTS FOR SLEEPING UNDER THE SUMMER SKY.

When Fiona Hooper purchased a small island in Penobscot Bay, she had no plans to build on it. "I had the dream to have for the rest of my life a place of wildness, of windblown light and dazzling seas where I could come with my family and sleep on sun-warmed rocks, share meals, and swim in a cold, indigo sea," she says, poetically. "There was no dock, no source of fresh water, but there were two small beaches," she recalls, "one with a swimming lagoon, the other overlooked by an enormous osprey nest," as well as balsam and spruce trees, maples and birches. It reminded her of her childhood in South Africa, of school vacations spent in mountain cabins and beach huts without electricity, of the enchantment, she says, of living off the grid.

For fifteen summers, Fiona and her family camped on the island in tents, swimming in the sea, living simply. But the need to gently tend to the island's forest—which had been ravaged over the years by storms—led to the idea of another mindful intervention: building a home that could be just as off-grid but slightly more rooted.

With a strict budget, Fiona and her husband, Tony Hooper, approached architect Sheila Bonnell, with whom they'd worked before. Their vision: an uninsulated, seasonal house that would provide simple, minimal shelter for summers otherwise lived outdoors. "It was to be built like a wooden boat: tight and able to stand up to forceful and shifting elements," Fiona says. The design takes cues from the nautical,

she adds, with "clean, sail-like angles and traditional maritime black-stained shiplap walls" inspired by the vernacular of fishing camps and boat sheds. There are wide decks, space-saving built-in furniture, and an outdoor shower that operates with heated rainwater—"essential for a family of cold-water swimmers," Fiona notes.

Still, summers here are much the same as they were during those first camping days: packing up the skiff with provisions, harvesting dinner from the kitchen garden, and bedding down on tent platforms around the island when the extended family comes to stay.

I

I Simple shelter
The house is built into a granite ledge and is completely off-grid, equipped with a solar panel, a generator, and a rainwater collection system.

2 Decks as living space
Weathered mahogany platforms connect the main room, bedroom, and studio, and create open-air spaces between, like this outdoor dining room, with a table draped in a cloth from the Conran Shop.

3 Think local
These salt-glazed mugs with rope handles are from Portland-based Objet Aimée.

4 Stacked storage
A trio of wooden crates is a movable, small-space substitute for a coffee table.

5 Sleek centerpiece
The Shaker woodstove from
Rockport-based Smith & May
provides extra warmth on
chilly offshore summer nights.
"We waited three years for it
to receive regulatory approval,
and its installation was cause for
celebration," says Fiona.

6 Fixed furniture
A built-in sofa by local builder
Fred Mazzoni is fitted with cushions
upholstered in indigo-dyed linen
sheets from Marston House (see
page 122).

7 Hidden cargo hold
Drawers underneath the couch are
used to stash spare table linens and
serving dishes. "As on a boat, the
available storage imposes a welcome
limit on how much of anything we
have with us here," says Fiona.

8

8 Cooking off-grid
Fiona worked with a supplier in
Rockport to find well-designed
gas appliances that do not require
electricity, like a Miele dishwasher
and a Viking range.

9 Camp kitchen
The stripped-back prep space has
hardy maple butcher-block counters.
Niches in the studs hold ceramics
and jars of homemade preserves.

10 Dinner by candlelight
Fiona found the dining table—a
vintage vintner's picnic table—in the
south of France. "It's comfortable for
a party as well as just two of us," she
says. The French folding chairs are
from Marston House.

9

11

11 No-tech AC
In the bedroom, French doors open to the outdoors for cool breezes off the water.

12 Sun shades
Simple roll-up linen blinds from Marston House cover the casement windows in the studio.

13 Extra berth
A daybed can sleep overnight guests when needed. In an off-grid house, a flashlight is a necessary bedside accoutrement.

14 Low-waste bath
"There is one flushing toilet and a hand basin in a tiny bathroom," says Fiona. Outdoors is a shower that uses heated rainwater; the grandchildren grew up bathing in large garden trugs on the deck.

12

13

14

15 Island life

"I wanted a place to be sometimes with our children and grandchildren and other times just us," says Fiona: "down at the dock, out on the boat, swimming the length of the island with the loons alongside, walking up the trail at dusk with mackerel for supper."

How to Dress for Summer in Style

KAZEEM LAWAL IS THE ALWAYS-DAPPER MAN-ABOUT-TOWN BEHIND PORTLAND TRADING CO., THE WELL-CURATED DOWNTOWN PORTLAND SHOP. BORN IN CALIFORNIA AND RAISED IN LAGOS, NIGERIA, KAZEEM MIXES MAINE STAPLES WITH GLOBAL FINDS. HERE ARE HIS FIVE TIPS FOR DRESSING FOR THE FOG, BREEZE, AND MIDDAY HEAT OF A MAINE SUMMER.

1 **Layer up.** "Winters are long here, and summers are short, so we try to enjoy as much time as possible outside in the warm months. Layering is key: Wear less during the day, then bundle up slightly at night as the light ocean chill sets in."

2 **Pay homage to the sea.** Work in bits of blue—nods to the summer skies and ocean.

3 **Add in a Maine standby or two.** Kazeem's go-tos: "Alden tassel loafers, a double-breasted navy linen blazer, and a Portland Trading Co. adventure tote bag."

4 **Be ready for anything.** "You never know where the day will take you: sailing, or for a lobster roll lunch or dinner at a restaurant. You can't go wrong with a fresh white Oxford shirt, a Harrington jacket, sunglasses, khaki shorts or linen pants, a vintage dress watch. And no socks."

5 **Keep it cool and casual.** When in doubt, "Cotton, cotton, cotton."

North Haven

THE GALLERISTS' HOUSE

A SEVENTH-GENERATION MAINER
AND A SCOTTISH ARTIST LIVE AND
WORK IN A NINETEENTH-CENTURY
GENERAL STORE AND CARRIAGE
HOUSE, A STONE'S THROW FROM
THE TOWN FERRY LANDING.

Make the passage to North Haven on the charmingly old-fashioned ferry and you can see David Wilson and David Hopkins's small stand of buildings—actually called Hopkins Wharf—ahead of you, jutting out over the water, the first signal that you've made it to the island.

Hopkins can tell you the story of each structure by heart—the wharf has been in his family since 1899. What was once his great-grandfather's general store, which sold "not only groceries but ice, gasoline, heating fuel, coal, lumber, and building supplies" and served as a chandlery for boats passing through, is now a gift shop with an apartment above. Next door is the former grain shed; it's now a gallery, with a studio above where Wilson, an artist, paints while looking out at the harbor. The onetime icehouse, where ice from the island's freshwater pond was cut to be delivered directly to villagers' pantries, is now an extension of the gallery. And the old carriage house, built on granite piers over the water, is the couple's living space.

Hopkins was raised on North Haven, in the apartment above what was then his mother's gift shop. But he can trace his Down East lineage even further back than the wharf, to one Dr. Theophilus Hopkins, who moved to Maine from Massachusetts in the late 1700s. David Wilson, meanwhile, is Scottish; the two met in London and lived in New York (Hopkins ran the Met's gift shop) before settling on the island in 2011 to preside over the shop and the art gallery. Now, in the one-room carriage house, the couple lives among antique finds, ephemera passed down through generations, pieces from artist friends, and breezes off the water.

1

1 Shipshape butcher block
"My brother Eric lived in the carriage house first, and he put the kitchen counter in during the late seventies or early eighties," says Hopkins. Shelves between wall studs display dishes and curiosities, like a triangular pennant from the local North Haven Casino yacht club. "It's for winning a dinghy race. I got it from a friend, who won it in the 1940s or '50s," Hopkins says.

2 Original landline
The couple still used the vintage rotary phone—once the only phone in the apartment over the store, says Hopkins—until they switched to fiber-optic cable. Above the phone is a reproduction of *LOVE* by Robert Indiana, who lived and worked in nearby Vinalhaven.

3 Cottage classic
Blue-and-white-striped linens are a must in a seaside house.

4 Storied objects
On display: a hook-handled broom, a hand-crank fire alarm from Hopkins's great-aunt's barn, and a nineteenth-century ship instrument used to measure distance. "My great-great-grandfather used it as a navigational aid when he sailed around Cape Horn," says Hopkins.

2

3

4

5 Low profile
A bench tucked beneath a window holds art books and keeps sight lines open.

6 Water view
"Unfortunately, our favorite thing about the house is now gone," says Hopkins. "Before the new floor was installed, we had a hatch opening to the water below. After dinner, we would often throw scraps down to the eels and crabs."

7 Open-air living
Latched double doors, installed by the Davids, open out onto the harbor and let in the salt air.

8 In the rafters
The original beams were left unpainted, to rustic effect.

9 Unfussy seating
An armchair adds a touch of Scotland to the space, with a braided seat cushion and woven blanket.

10 Citronella as sculpture
A citronella coil in a corner of the
living room looks abstract and artful
(and keeps summer bugs at bay).

11 Built-in storage
The exposed studs create a
convenient place to stash umbrellas
and boat paddles. The ladder leads
to the couple's sleeping loft.

13

14

12 Paneled pantry
Next door, in the apartment above the gift shop, a dark wood-clad passageway leads to the kitchen beyond.

13 Artful spaces
The dining room in the apartment was once the telephone office and switchboard for the whole island. The artwork is by Hopkins's brother Eric.

14 Textural backdrop
The piano once belonged to Hopkins's mother. Note the rustic patinated walls.

16

17

15 The ideal summer bedroom
A guest room above the shop is outfitted simply, with a white cotton coverlet and a pair of binoculars.

16 Deconstructed WC
"The marble sink is original to the building when it was built between 1899 and 1901," says Hopkins. "I remember taking baths in the old tin bathtub, since replaced."

17 Ad hoc display
A cabinet and vintage mirror transform an unused doorway. The branch in the bowl is a bit of found sculpture.

18 Waterside perch
The couple's carriage-house quarters. "We jacked it up 18 inches in the 1990s to allow for the threat of rising tides due to climate change," says Hopkins; the water passes underneath.

19 Attic atelier
Wilson's painting studio is above the gallery, with uninterrupted views of the water.

20 Island art space
Hopkins Wharf Gallery, once the grain shed.

How to Survive Summer sans AC

SHARON AND PAUL MROZINSKI SPEND WINTERS IN FRANCE AND SUMMERS ON VINALHAVEN, WHERE THEY LIVE ABOVE THEIR TREASURE-FILLED ANTIQUES SHOP, MARSTON HOUSE (SEE PAGE 122). "OUR HOME SITS ON A NATURAL GRANITE ISLAND; THREE SIDES ARE SURROUNDED BY THE SEA," SAYS SHARON. AS IN MOST MAINE HOMES, THERE'S NO AIR-CONDITIONING. HERE ARE FOUR OF THEIR GO-TO METHODS FOR KEEPING COOL.

1 Encourage air movement. Open windows across from each other to get a cross breeze all day. "We leave the windows open twenty-four hours and absolutely love this natural cooling," says Sharon. On still days, keep the windows shut until you can enjoy the cool evening air.

2 Sport a cool cloth. At the couple's previous home in Wiscasset, Maine, "when the only air movement was Route One traffic," Sharon would tie a wet bandanna or rag around her neck for an easy refresh. It's a simple trick that works wonders—see page 118 for a slightly elevated version.

3 Live in linen. "Sleeping on and under linen sheets is incredibly cooling," says Sharon. "Linen naturally absorbs any moisture in the air and on your body." For laundering, "fresh air is always ideal—clotheslines are required at our home."

4 Take a plunge. "A cold shower is the best quick fix. Or a dive into the sea or fresh moving water (swimming pools have too many chemicals). Enjoy the cold water and soak it in. Your body will thank you."

THE ENVIRONMENTALIST'S HOUSE

ON THE EDGE OF MAINE,
A TRAILBLAZING LAND
ADVOCATE IS CREATING A
TEMPLATE FOR THE FUTURE.

Severine von Tscharner Fleming first came to Maine for the seaweed: specifically, to harvest algae from the rocky shores at muddy low tides. She's now a filmmaker, a farmer, a founder of no fewer than four organizations, the publisher of a literary journal called *The New Farmer's Almanac*, and, still, a seaweed cultivator, just to name a few of the hats she wears. She even arranges mixers for young landworkers: "I try to discern what is needed and what will help those who are newly joining the organic movement as farmers," she says.

She's also a salvager. In Maine's northeasternmost reaches, Severine has purchased a collection of old structures— a disused community hall, a motel—with the intent of fixing them up with local and found materials to save them and, by extension, preserve the land around them.

If Severine's mission centers on one span of land in particular, though, it's Smithereen Farm, on a peninsula overlooking Cobscook Bay in northern Maine near the Canadian border. Here a team of young farmers harvest seaweed, wild apples, and fish, and make tinctures, salves, ciders, and teas from herbs and flowers. The farm hosts artists, poets, climate pioneers, blueberry pickers, and campers, who can book a tent platform via Airbnb. (A stay includes access to the outdoor shower and seaweed soaks in cast-iron bathtubs under the apple trees.) At the center of the gardens is an 1820s farmhouse, a yurt, and an open-air, timber-frame summer kitchen where Smithereen farmers live, work, and cook as a community.

"The farmhouse was renovated by Maine Farmland trust before I got here" and saved from neglect, says Severine. But her spirit has transformed it into a space of activity and creativity. Rooms are filled with hand-me-down and found furniture and bundles of wild-foraged herbs, and the camplike kitchen is open to all who pass through. "We have what we need: the wind, the fish, the rivers, the forests, the botanicals, the wild blueberries," Severine says. "This is a place of abundance at the far north of New England."

1

1 Land's end
The shingled farmhouse sits on the tip of a peninsula. "It's like being on a ship," says Severine. "It's all about the wind and the weather and the wildness."

2 Farm kitchen
The stripped-back farmhouse kitchen has painted wood floors and a collection of furniture, planks, and carts that serve as counters.

4

3 Team building
"I got the sink from a junk shop,"
says Severine. A Smithereen farmer
built the foundation for it, and
another built the draining rack. A
super-simple sink skirt hides all sorts
of kitchen extras, and nails above
the sink make handy places to hang
scissors and scrubbers.

4 Farm to counter
Smithereen's offerings are wide-
ranging: pickles, apple butter, hard
cider, salves made from herbs
and beeswax, blueberry jam, and
foraged Chaga.

5 DIY standing desk
One farmworker's ad hoc desk
consists of a large plank of wood atop
extra Warré beehives "made by our
friend the beekeeper," Severine says.
A jar of apple cider vinegar doubles
as work-space decor, and a chain of
dried marigolds—used for dyeing
cloth—hangs from the window.

5

6

7

8

6 Preserving the old
Severine is working to salvage buildings in this northeastern bit of Maine, including a dark-clad community hall with original lights.

7 Maine vignette
Sea urchins and a feather are on display with a framed letterpress print, part of a series of limited-edition posters by Wolfe Editions in Portland celebrating the coast of Maine; this one was for the bicentennial of the town of Lubec.

8 All-natural air freshener
A thicket of the herb Sweet Annie adds wildness—and a pleasant scent—to a corner of the living room. "It's great for keeping away flies," says Severine. "There's a whole category of herbs called 'strewing herbs,' which were big in the Middle Ages when people and animals lived on top of each other, as we do at Smithereen Farm."

9 Layered living
A sheepskin adds casual coziness to a settee from Severine's grandmother's house. "You can find all the lovely sheepskins you'd ever want at the Common Ground Country Fair, held every year by the Maine Organic Farmers and Gardeners Association," Severine says of the hides on display throughout the house.

11

10 Creative reuse
"We buy from junk shops, yard sales, the community flea market in Machias. We adopt things from the side of the road," says Severine of the collected, repurposed, and upcycled furnishings.

11 Shades of blue
An antique hutch, vintage lamp, dark sheepskin, and gray-painted floors create a moody, high-contrast palette in one farmworker's bedroom.

12 A play on scale
A heavy wooden sleigh bed anchors the room. Severine collected the mix-and-match linens throughout the farmhouse from thrift stores and French flea markets.

12

13 Just the essentials
The prep space in the open-air kitchen is outfitted with baskets, shelves for storing jars, and a cloth tacked on the window frame to keep out the sun.

14 Washing-up station
A wall-mounted outdoor sink is available "for visiting campers to brush their teeth," Severine says.

15 Summer kitchen
A farmer works in the timber-frame structure made by builder Raivo Vihman of Haystack Joinery and builder and stonemason Vidar Zay.

16 With the tides

The farm overlooks Cobscook Bay.
"Cobscook means 'boiling water'
in the Passamaquoddy language,"
says Severine. "The nearby falls
reverse direction depending on
the tide, creating seventeen acres
of churning water. It's the central
metaphor for our project here,
where change is possible."

17

18

19

17 Yurt living
Severine lives near the farmhouse in a yurt that is built in the style of Bill Coperthwaite, the architect and homesteader often called the Thoreau of Maine.

18 Iconic dessert
Blueberry pie is a Maine summer must-have.

19 Free range
The Smithereen grounds are open to the community for wild blueberry picking and late-summer-night revelry.

20 Family style
Height-of-summer dinners are sometimes taken outdoors, at a weathered picnic table set with enamelware and checkered napkins.

How to Create Vignettes from Beach-Walk Finds

MICHELLE PROVENÇAL
IS THE THIRD-GENERATION
MAINER BEHIND THIRDLEE
& CO., THE ONLINE SHOP
WHERE SHE SELLS HER
FINELY DETAILED HANDMADE
ORNAMENTS INSPIRED BY THE
SEA. "I CAN'T LEAVE THE BEACH
WITHOUT SOMETHING IN MY
POCKET," SHE SAYS. "USUALLY
IT'S A SHELL OR A BIT OF
DRIFTWOOD, MAYBE A CURL
OF BIRCH BARK THAT SPENT
TIME ROLLING AROUND IN THE
SURF." SHE DISPLAYS HER FINDS
IN HER WALDOBORO STUDIO
WITH A DEFT TOUCH AND
THESE FIVE TRICKS IN MIND.

1 Go by shape. "As a
product designer, I am drawn
to sculptural pieces like sea
sponges, large conch shells, and
driftwood, and see them as
artwork in their own right." Let
standout silhouettes shine on
their own.

2 Make miniature displays.
Create stories from specimens;
for example, "a glass cloche with
a few found treasures from one
walk on the beach."

3 Branch out. "I love using
branches, specifically driftwood
and manzanita, as decor. Cured
and sandblasted, they feel

wild and beachy. Several in a
large vase add drama, but
laying a single branch down
the center of the table makes a
sculptural centerpiece."

4 Follow a formula. "Line +
plane + mass: a simple formula
for a visually interesting vignette.
Think a branch, a stack of vintage
books, and a shell."

5 Mix materials. "Pair contrasting
finishes, like a polished smooth
stone with a piece of rough
driftwood. It creates tension
(in a good way)."

Bait Bag Soap Holder

Evidence of the state's robust lobster industry, nylon bait bags can be found all along Maine's rocky shores. Mainers like to repurpose these colorful pouches as suet feeders for birds or as easy DIY doorstops (simply insert a stone, as shown below). No washed-up nets handy where you are? We fashioned our own net bag using natural yarn and simple, hand-tied knots to create a soap hanger that doubles as a scrubber in an outdoor (or indoor) shower.

Bait Bag Soap Holder

MATERIALS

RULER OR MEASURING TAPE

SCISSORS

LINEN, HEMP, OR COTTON
YARN

4-INCH EMBROIDERY HOOP

1 Gather your materials.

2 Measure and cut eighteen
36-inch pieces of yarn. Fold
one strand in half over the
embroidery hoop and loosely
tie with an overhand loop knot:
Take hold of the two strings just
under the hoop with one hand,
grab the hanging yarn about
2 inches under this point and
bring it up to form a loop. Then
thread the end over and under
through the loop and pull tight.
Repeat with the remaining
seventeen strings, making sure
the knots are equidistant from
the hoop, then spread the
knotted strings evenly around
the hoop.

3 Take one strand from the first
knot and one from the adjacent
knot and tie them together with
another overhand loop knot,
about ¼ inch below the first
row of knots. Repeat along the
row, making sure to keep the
length and spacing consistent;
tie the last string in the row to
the first to complete the circle.
Continue this process, tying
each new row about ¼ inch
below the row you've just
completed, until you have eight
knotted rows (for a small soap)
or ten (for a large bar).

4 For the final row, instead
of pulling the yarn all the way
through the knot, leave each as
a loop. Trim the excess string.

5 Remove the netted bag from
the embroidery hoop. Thread
one end with a piece of yarn,
tie closed, and trim.

6 Thread the other end with a
longer piece of yarn (doubled,
for strength) for cinching and
hanging your bait bag.

1

2

3

4

5

6

Simple Cooling Cloths

There's much to be admired about the Lost Kitchen, Erin French's famed restaurant in Freedom, Maine (including her lush flower arrangements—see page 30). In addition to the just-gathered food and streamside perch, little details such as refreshing cooling cloths complete the intimate dining experience. Happily, Erin and Nancy Buckley, a member of the all-woman team who prepares them on hot summer nights, agreed to share their recipe with us. The Lost Kitchen uses linen cloths, but we used antique damask napkins.

MATERIALS

⅔ CUP ROSE WATER
(STORE-BOUGHT OR
HOMEMADE—SEE NOTE)

BOWL

LINEN OR COTTON NAPKINS
OR CLOTHS

TWINE

LAVENDER SPRIGS (FRESH OR
DRIED)

1 Lay each napkin or cloth flat, facedown, and fold lengthwise so that the ends meet in the middle, like a pair of French doors. Fold lengthwise in half. Roll each cloth tightly.

2 In a bowl, mix ⅔ cup each of rose water and tap water. Place each roll in the mixture until fully saturated. Remove and gently squeeze out the excess liquid.

3 Tie each rolled cloth with a bit of twine (we chose natural linen), and insert a sprig of fresh or dried lavender. Keep in an airtight container until ready to use. If it's quite hot out, refrigerate for added cooling.

1

2

3

NOTE: To make your own rose water, simply place garden rose petals (store-bought roses aren't sufficiently fragrant) in a pan and pour in just enough distilled water to cover. Bring to a simmer, reduce the heat to low, and cook for about 15 minutes, until the petals lose their color. Remove from the heat and let sit until cool. Or you can substitute dried roses, using a ratio of ¼ cup petals to 1½ cups distilled water.

Where to Go in Warm Weather

Among the lobster shacks, beaches, and state parks, there's no shortage of design-forward inns, restaurants, galleries, and shops to visit in Maine's brief but glorious warm season, both along the coast and everywhere in between; consider this our shortlist of don't-miss stops, from south to north. Because Maine is such a seasonal state, double-check opening hours, then trace a route with your old-fashioned road atlas and head out. For more on these destinations, see Resources, beginning on page 210.

SNUG HARBOR FARM
Kennebunk

Stop into this tucked-away nursery for hand-thrown, appealingly patinated terra-cotta pots and good-looking gardening essentials; stay to wander the *Secret Garden*-esque grounds and peek into the dovecote.

WINSLOW HOMER STUDIO
Scarborough

The Portland Museum of Art preserves this dark-clad house and studio on the tip of Prouts Neck where Winslow Homer lived and painted from 1883 to 1910. Homer enlisted famed Maine architect John Calvin Stevens to renovate the carriage house; the second-floor deck offers uninterrupted views of the rocky coast, a familiar sight from Homer's work. Visits are by guided tour only.

SABBATHDAY LAKE SHAKER VILLAGE
New Gloucester

We've long admired the Shakers for their simple utilitarian wares (see: peg rails, boxes, brooms), and it just so happens that the last active Shaker community in the world is in Maine. Tours visit village buildings and exhibits on design and history; don't forget to stop by the shop, too.

SEVEN LAKES INN
↑ *Belgrade*

The lakeside lodge gets an upgrade in this four-room 1840s farmhouse, redone by a mother-daughter team. Their design-forward but easygoing sensibility is on full display, from the white-painted floors and natural-fiber rugs to the heirloom quilts in each guest bedroom.

TOPS'L FARM
Waldoboro

This glamping spot has the feel of an extremely well-appointed summer camp. Individual cabins are outfitted with luxe linens, lanterns, and sheepskins; ask ahead and the team will pack a vintage cooler with provisions for a picnic.

SUGAR TOOLS
Camden

Inevitably, each time we ask a Maine homeowner where they sourced a perfect iron hook or basket, we get the same answer: Sugar Tools.

The small shop carries impeccably made essentials (hanging onion baskets, soap dishes) and elevated extras (brass hairpins, cotton sleep masks).

LINCOLNVILLE MOTEL
Lincolnville

We love the stripped-back summer simplicity of this redone 1950s motel, with whitewashed walls, Donald Judd-esque plywood headboards, record players, and canvas drop cloth shades on every window.

THE LOST KITCHEN
← *Freedom*

This is one of the country's most-talked-about restaurants, but you'll need to mail a love letter—and wind through back roads—to find it. Chef Erin French hosts one seating a night from May through October in an old mill perched over a stream, complete with flowers she arranges herself (see her tips on page 30). How to get a reservation? Mail a postcard on April 1 and hope your name gets drawn.

CHASE'S DAILY
Belfast

This bakery, self-described "fledgling restaurant," and miniature greenmarket sells produce and beautifully arranged bundles of flowers, all freshly picked from the family farm in Freedom.

TURNER FARM AND NEBO LODGE
North Haven

This organic island farm owned by political powerhouse Chellie Pingree hosts a series of suppers in a timber-frame barn and runs a farm stand, too. Stay nearby at Nebo Lodge, a nine-room inn and restaurant renovated by Pingree, with painted wood floors and vintage iron beds.

HOPKINS WHARF GALLERY AND NORTH HAVEN GIFT SHOP
North Haven

David Hopkins and David Wilson's gallery near the ferry landing shows the work of artists with connections to North Haven and Vinalhaven; stop in to the gift shop next door—a longtime island favorite—for curated Maine classics (balsam pillows and books by local writers, from Susan Minot to Elizabeth Bishop) as well as unexpected finds, such as bright Indian-printed napkins. (See Hopkins and Wilson's own space on page 81.)

MARSTON HOUSE
→ *Vinalhaven*

Sharon and Paul Mrozinski spend half the year scouring the South of France for antique ceramics, ticking cloth, and homespun linens—the more patched and lovingly mended, the better—then sell them, come summer, in the chock-full shop below their island apartment. (For more on the couple's love of linen, see page 95.)

GOOD LIFE CENTER
← *Harborside*

Forest Farm—with its stone house, walled gardens, greenhouse, and library—was the last home of pioneering sustainable-living activists Helen and Scott Nearing, where they lived simply, off the land. It's now preserved as the Good Life Center, with the homestead open for tours and a lecture series, too.

shop follows suit with vintage nautical wares and curios as well as owner Tim Whitten's hand-done ropework and knots.

THE BROOKLIN INN
← *Brooklin*

"A classic Maine inn with a modern approach": That's how the team behind this tiny four-room guesthouse on the Blue Hill Peninsula describes it. Here, textural walls and muted hues mix with collected paintings and blooms from the grounds. (Not too far away: the private farm where E. B. White lived and wrote *Charlotte's Web*.)

ABBE MUSEUM
Bar Harbor

The only Smithsonian affiliate in the state, the Abbe Museum explores the history of the Wabanaki people (the original inhabitants of the land now called Maine), with a core collection as well as exhibits of Wabanaki basketry, objects, and innovations. The smaller trailside museum is nearby at Sieur de Monts Spring in Acadia National Park.

ARAGOSTA AT GOOSE COVE
Deer Isle

These bright oceanside cottages are uncommonly cheerful, with seafoam-painted floors, striped linens, and tiny but well-fitted kitchenettes. The celebrated restaurant and lodgings alike are finished with local makers' wares, from the communal table and tiles behind the reception desk down to the servers' aprons.

HAYSTACK MOUNTAIN SCHOOL OF CRAFTS
→ *Deer Isle*

Worth the drive for the architecture alone, this shingled, angular-roofed arts campus designed by Edward Larrabee Barnes and listed on the National Register of Historic Places is set into the craggy, pine-studded coastal landscape. Stop in for a craft presentation or a guided tour of working artists' studios.

MARLINESPIKE CHANDLERY
Stonington

A chandlery traditionally sold essentials for ships and boats, and this nautical bric-a-brac

NEW SWEDEN HISTORICAL SOCIETY
New Sweden

Taking part in a Swedish midsommar celebration might not seem like standard Maine fare, but travel northward at the summer solstice and you'll find bright folk attire, flower crowns, and a maypole, traditions carried on by descendants of Swedes who arrived here in 1870. All with a Down East twist, that is: Maine lupines are woven among the wildflowers.

Thistle

Autumn

Vinalhaven

THE DECONSTRUCTED GUESTHOUSE

ON THE CRAGGY SITE OF A FORMER QUARRY, A EUROPEAN COUPLE BUILT A TRIO OF SMALL, INTERCONNECTED CABINS FOR THEIR FAR-FLUNG FAMILY.

"This is our escape spot," says designer Nadja Zerunian of a small cluster of cabins perched on a remote parcel on Vinalhaven. "It's far removed from our daily lives and routines in Europe, where we spend the rest of the year." Nadja is Austrian and her husband, Nick van Praag, is British, and a few years ago they found themselves in search of a quiet spot somewhere in the world to retreat to—"somewhere we could reunite our peripatetic family," Nadja says. "Whenever we were on the verge of closing, Nick said, 'But you should see Maine first.'" So the pair traveled west, to Vinalhaven, and stayed at a distant relative's place. On the trip, "I got sick," Nadja says. "I guess I was a bit too cold and definitely underdressed for the beach vacation I had imagined." Still, she says, "I fell in love with this rough gem of an island. The fir trees reminded me of my childhood in Austria, and the permanent chill and the promise of messing around in boats was, I guess, what finally ticked all the boxes for my British husband."

The couple first purchased a small modernist house on stilts on the island (built in the 1960s by a student and then partner of Walter Gropius), then bought the adjacent property, a former quarry, and commissioned neighbor and friend Riley Pratt of Belfast-based OPAL Architecture to build separate guest quarters on it.

The "guesthouse" is actually three small, peaked structures, set gently into the landscape. One holds the living area and kitchen, the other two a bed and bath each; all three are connected by cedar walkways and decks. "Nick always complains about getting wet when going for a cup of tea, but he should be used to the rain," Nadja jokes. The interiors are spare and sculptural, with natural-fiber rugs, washi paper Noguchi lights, and peg rails displaying bric-a-brac found on island walks. Added into the textural mix are clean-lined mid-century classics, finds from Maine flea markets and antiques shops, and lots of stones, Nadja's obsession. "We love the simplicity that Maine suggests and that island life demands, where one brings only the essentials," she says. The buildings are not winterized, but there's a sleek woodstove for warmth on cool nights and early-autumn days.

The guesthouses are a practical place for the couple's children and grandchildren to gather together, and for Nadja and Nick, the magic of the guesthouses is in their ephemerality. "It's the feeling that you have reached the end of the world and that you can pick blackberries while lying on the deck. And that you can close the houses up and dream about them for another year."

|

2

3

1 Collected objects

A woodstove stands in the corner of the living room. To its right are a pair of wooden skinning boards; a vintage cylindrical boat weight; and, on the floor, an antique Japanese leather headrest. On the wall is a paper bag with a child's drawing on it that the couple found on the beach.

2 Stockpot stockpile

"I used to be obsessed with old cast-iron pots," says Nadja. "They're such iconic shapes, and I bought a lot of them for storage."

3 Biting humor

Opposite the living area is a simple kitchen. The shark on the wall is Nadja's self-deprecating inside joke, a nod to her greatest phobia.

4 Natural palette
In the sparely appointed living area, neutral hues echo the wild land just outside the windows. "We're committed to the American tradition of the inside/outside feeling of spaces," Nadja says.

5 Extended living space
Floor-to-ceiling sliding doors open onto the cedar walkways.

6 Tough textiles
A natural-fiber rug is hardy and fuss-free for the guest cottage.

7 Modern hearth
A mid-century Preway fireplace sits atop a slab of heat-treated local Vinalhaven granite. ("It took quite a few very strong guys to deliver it," Nadja says.)

8 Shades of pale
The walls are painted in Benjamin Moore's Paper White, the floors in high-gloss Toplac boat paint. (For a similar paint we recommend, see page 206.)

9

9 Budget kitchen
"The kitchen is IKEA. All the cabinets have a pullout function, and I used uniform fronts to calm the room," says Nadja. The fronts also conceal an undercounter fridge and dishwasher.

10 Old Maine
An iron ring from Marlinespike Chandlery in Stonington (see page 123) and a rusted axe-head Nadja found while clearing brush are displayed on a sideboard alongside a Shaker stool from Trillium Soaps in Rockland (see page 201). Washi paper Noguchi lights appear throughout the space: "I love their fragility and the light they cast," says Nadja.

11 Beauty in utility
Baskets beneath a nineteenth-century Swedish sideboard store mosquito repellent, sunscreen, flashlights, linens, and more collected stones, stashed away by Nadja.

10

11

12

13

12 Low-impact lumber
The architects opted for cross-laminated timber panels made of layers of hardy black spruce, precut and prefabricated to facilitate transport by truck and ferry to the island.

13 Morning vistas
Cedar walkways lead to the guest rooms, where wraparound sliding doors offer sweeping views of the landscape from bed.

14 Fuss-free linens
A bedroom in one of the tiny guest cabins, with stripy seersucker bedding from IKEA—no ironing needed.

15 Island time
The only way to get to Vinalhaven is by boat or ferry. "There is no cell phone reception on most of the island; people greet each other on the streets," says Nadja. "It's almost like going through a time machine."

14

15

How to Prepare Wood for the Fire

GARDNER WALDEIER IS BETTER KNOWN IN MAINE BY HIS ALIAS, BUS HUXLEY, AND HIS EPONYMOUS YOUTUBE CHANNEL. THERE, HE CHRONICLES CAN-DO TASKS IN THE MAINE WOODS: BUILDING A TIMBER-FRAME HOUSE USING TREES FROM HIS PROPERTY IN WATERFORD, SPLITTING GRANITE BOULDERS, AND LAYING STONE WALLS. HERE ARE HIS FOUR LESSONS ON READYING A SUPPLY OF FIREWOOD FOR THE LONG WINTER AHEAD.

1 **Source.** "Black locust, oak, sugar maple, and beech are best for burning; Norway maple, red maple, poplar, and white birch are lower on the list but still good." Meanwhile, "softwoods, or coniferous trees—like white or red pine, hemlock, spruce, and balsam fir—burn hot and fast and are great for kindling."

2 **Split.** "With the right tool, a straight-grained, knot-free chunk of oak can be tackled with ease. A personal favorite is the maul, which has been used for as long as wood has been split."

3 **Stack.** "For years, I used a squeaky old metal wheelbarrow to cart firewood from the woodpile to the woodshed of our 220-year-old farmhouse. In performing such a strenuous task, I've realized the importance of the placement of the wood pile." Stack your wood within reasonable walking distance of your front door, and make sure to have good airflow and coverage to dry (season) it. "An age-old trick is orienting your wood stack with a compass so the end-grain faces east–west, maximizing exposure to the sun."

4 **Store.** "Indoors, keep logs close to where you'll ultimately burn them (but a safe distance from your stove or fireplace). To avoid bugs and moisture, stack in a covered, well-ventilated space."

Cape Elizabeth

THE YOUNG CREATIVES' HOUSE

LESS THAN TEN MILES FROM PORTLAND'S HAPPENING CENTER, AN ARCHITECT OPENED UP A RUN-DOWN SIXTIES BUNGALOW THAT SHE SHARES WITH HER DJ HUSBAND AND THEIR TODDLER SON.

When Jocie Dickson, the architect behind Jocelyn O Dickson Architecture, and her husband, Graham Dickson, a musician and DJ, decamped from New York City after a decade, they both felt pulled toward the ocean: Graham is a surfer and grew up on Nantucket; Jocie has family in Maine. In their search for a place of their own, they found a true rarity: a house by the sea in Cape Elizabeth, a quiet town minutes away from Portland known for its spectacular state parks.

The 1969 bungalow, though, was in bad shape. "The house had been built by the former owner," says Jocie, "and his approach to making changes and dealing with issues was very much 'put a Band-Aid on it.' The basement walls were filled with packing peanuts for insulation; the sunroom skylights had been covered with vinyl flooring."

But Jocie was eager for the challenge of transforming the seriously dated interiors—opening up walls, organizing spaces around a central staircase, and gutting the kitchen and baths—as a project for her young family and her new firm, too. "I thought about the climate of Maine a lot, as the space needed to feel cozy during the cold, white winters but also light and airy during the verdant summers," she says. "For me, white walls with natural accents create the perfect canvas for adding color with textiles, artwork, and furnishings"—some inherited from family, and all kid-friendly for the couple's son, Zephyr.

The house is situated on a dirt road at the edge of a suburban neighborhood. "There is a spectacular walking path in front of the house that follows the shoreline," says Jocie. "From there, you can access magical rocky coves and patches of wild strawberries and blueberries." The family works on their own parcel of land in bits and pieces, planting apple trees and uncovering natural blackberry and raspberry thickets and bayberry bushes. "Ultimately, we'd like the landscape to feel quite wild and unmanicured, like it's an extension of the rocky shore."

1

1 Music room
The "sunroom" on the main floor houses the couple's collection of vinyl (including rare editions from Jocie's grandfather, who worked in the record industry). "Graham almost exclusively plays records when DJing," Jocie says. The interiors are painted in a color match of Benjamin Moore's Decorator's White.

2 Hidden storage
Built-in benches along one wall in the sunroom serve as seating and an extra place to stash essentials. Inside? "Oversize kitchen items (like a lobster pot) and our projector screen, which we hang in front of the windows on small J hooks," says Jocie.

3 Key element

"We moved the piano into the house pre-renovation, when Graham was using the space as a studio, so it lived through the whole construction process," says Jocie.

4 Kid-friendly zone
Baskets keep Zephyr's toys within easy reach.

5 The power of paint
The redbrick fireplace was painted white, to sculptural, minimal effect.

6 Reimagined fireplace
Art, architecture books, and vases of flowers now fill the repurposed structure.

9

7 Open concept
To brighten up the dark interiors, Jocie demoed the walls dividing the dining room and sunroom. The paper lantern is by Hay, and the vintage Breuer Cesca chairs were Jocie's grandmother's.

8 Clear sight lines
Jocie redid the kitchen with IKEA cabinet boxes fitted with Reform fronts and black Richlite counters, and she opted for long windows instead of upper cabinets for a dishwashing spot with a view. The vintage rug is from Portia's Barn in Portland (see page 211). "The color of the kitchen cabinets—Vapour by Reform CPH—is very oceanic," says Jocie. "It changes dramatically with the light: Sometimes it's gray, and sometimes it looks very blue green."

9 Redone stairs
Jocie and Zephyr on the newly built stairway—now a connection point between all the levels in the house—with a screen of western red cedar. Before, the main connection between the floors was a narrow, precarious spiral stair.

10 Home studio

Jocie's office—in a nook off of the bedroom—is whitewashed and simple, with texture and pattern thanks to a sheepskin throw, woven lights, and a bundle of branches in one corner.

11 Streamlined sleep nook

The main bedroom is kept spare, with a bed from Floyd and twin Anglepoise Type 75 wall-mounted lights to save space.

12 Budget-friendly floors

"The whole third floor was carpeted with a shaggy emerald-green beauty, even in the bathroom," says Jocie. She installed new pine boards painted in Benjamin Moore's Chantilly Lace (more affordable than staining). "I liked the idea of a serene all-white space for our bedroom, and it was also the best place in the house for white floors: low traffic, mostly shoeless."

12

13

14

13 Unsightly to serene

The former bath was "crazy," says Jocie, with "a massive Jacuzzi tub and carpeted steps surrounding it." She built out a small WC, left the rest of the space open to the main bedroom, and opted for a spa-like suite of materials: Venetian plaster walls by Master of Plaster, a custom teak vanity she designed herself, and FLOS Glo-Ball lights by Jasper Morrison.

14 Big-box meets bespoke

The shower and bath area is fitted with wall tiles from Clé Tile, new windows, a custom teak tub surround, and slate floors from Home Depot.

15 Front-yard trails

Jocie and Zephyr on an evening autumn walk by the sea.

How to Hunt for Flea-Market Finds

CERAMICIST **HANAKO NAKAZATO** AND PHOTOGRAPHER/WRITER **PRAIRIE STUART-WOLFF** SPEND HALF THE YEAR IN THE PORT CITY OF KARATSU, JAPAN, AND HALF THE YEAR IN UNION, MAINE, WHERE THEIR HOME IS FILLED WITH VINTAGE AND SALVAGED FINDS SOURCED FROM FAVORITE HAUNTS ALL ALONG THE COAST. HERE ARE FIVE OF PRAIRIE'S POINTERS ON SCORING FLEA-MARKET GEMS.

1 Come prepared. "A check in your wallet means you'll never have to walk away from a great find if a vendor doesn't accept credit cards. And carry a tape measure: It will come in handy when you're trying to decide if that side table is the right size."

2 Do your research. Know what you're looking for. "When I decided to build a vintage cast-iron skillet collection, I familiarized myself with the logo and design details for the era of manufacturing that I wanted. That made it easier to go through stacks of skillets quickly."

3 Browse high. "Even when their offerings are out of your budget, visiting high-end dealers will train your eye. That way, you can spot quality items within the dusty heaps in antiques barns and junk shops."

4 Don't be put off by a little cleanup. A four-piece fix-up kit can tackle just about anything. "Keep a can of WD-40, 220-grit sandpaper, some mineral oil, and a bag of rags around to make metal shine again and spruce up anything made of wood."

5 Think beyond the obvious. "Old irons make great doorstops; a marble mantel propped up on two blocks of wood makes a perfect shoe shelf in the entry."

Fire-Starter Bundles

From summer marshmallow toasts to cozy autumn hearths, fires are a year-round activity Down East, so every Mainer knows how to light a good blaze. Fire starters really help and are especially pleasing when made of aromatic greenery. Seek out combustible and/or fragrant natural materials such as pinecones, pine branches, and birch bark.

MATERIALS

NATURAL TINDER

BIODEGRADABLE SEEDLING
POTS OR EGG CARTONS

WICKING

POT FOR MELTING WAX

BEESWAX

1 Take a short stroll into any woods and you'll quickly come up with enough foraged flora for your fire starters. We found dried old-man's beard (*Usnea*), pinecones, and birch bark (which are all rich in oil) as well as aromatic balsam firs and native sweet fern (*Comptonia peregrina*).

2 While recycled egg cartons make tidy, small versions ideal for camping, biodegradable seed starters create more generous fire starters for the home hearth.

Just be sure to plug the bottom hole with a small pinecone or acorn cap, or the hot wax will run out. Place a 2-inch piece of wick in your seedling pot or egg carton and artfully surround with your flammable finds.

3 Warm the wax on the stove on low heat until it's completely melted, then immediately remove and pour a small amount over each fire starter. Allow to dry; then set near your fireplace or package as gifts.

1

2

3

Mussel Shell Votives

Generously sized, with a rich indigo hue, Maine mussel shells are perfect for the coastal table. We've used them as impromptu pinch pots for salt and pepper or, as here, for easy votive candles. Scatter these tea lights down the center of the table or on the mantel to keep a bit of summer going through fall and beyond. (Don't have mussels on hand? Any substantial seashell will do.)

MATERIALS

MUSSEL SHELLS

POT FOR MELTING WAX

BEESWAX OR SOY WAX

PEBBLES OR SAND

VOTIVE WICKS

1 Gather mussel shells along the shore or save them from your last meal. Clean the shells and dry.

2 Warm the wax on low heat; once it's completely melted, immediately remove from the burner. (We like to use ethically sourced beeswax with its pretty amber color, which complements the mussels' deep blue, but you can use soy wax as well.)

3 The bottoms of mussels aren't often level; nestle them in a bed of pebbles (or sand) so they sit evenly while you fill them. Place a wick in each mussel, then carefully pour the wax over until it's just below the edge of the shell, and allow to dry. If your votives don't sit level on the table, stick a bit of softened wax to the bottom to stabilize them.

1

2

3

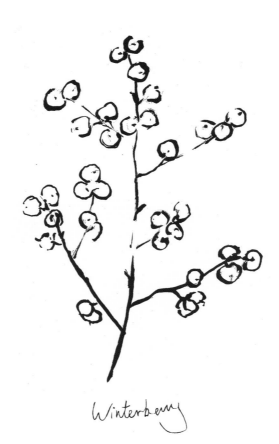

Winterberry

Winter

THE MAKERS' HOUSE

AN ARTIST, A DESIGNER, AND
THEIR TWO YOUNG CHILDREN LIVE
IN A SNUG, WOOD-HEATED HOUSE
BUILT ENTIRELY FROM SCRATCH.

Artist and builder Anthony Esteves and clothing designer Julie O'Rourke make most everything themselves: hand-painted candleholders in winter, pies filled with foraged berries in summer, and even their small charred-black house, timber barn, and wood-fired sauna on Spruce Head.

The structures are situated in a quiet clearing and evoke a rambling early–New England homestead—part of Anthony's inspiration. "The homes of the 1600s have a ghostly quality," he says. "They are defined by simplicity of shape and adornment and stand to be noticed in the landscape." It's a spirit evident in their home, aptly named Soot House. Anthony built the structure by hand, taking cues from the craggy landscape of black spruce and lichens; from Japanese techniques; and from his art training at Rhode Island

School of Design. "I treat the house as a sculpture," he says.

Inside, pared-back interiors and age-old details—plaster walls, eastern white cedar floors, windows that look out at the pines, and a woodstove for heat through the long, cold winters—are the backdrop for the family's endlessly creative spirit. The interiors are always shifting to accommodate making things or fit in a newly handmade object or found antique. "I think I can count on one hand all the 'new' things we have in our house," Julie says. "We mostly make things we need or collect them from yard sales and antiques stores, or from outside."

Flexibility is also required for living as a family of four (plus a dog) in the 560-square-foot space. Both of the couple's boys, Diogo and Rui, were born in the house, and it's become something of a modern one-room homestead. "It's important for us to have interiors that work with our reality; we are messy and not very gentle with things, and there is a lot of action in our small space." And a lot of inspired details, too.

I Vintage Maine
An old orchard ladder leans against the front wall of the main room.

2 By candlelight
The brass and copper sconces were found at a Brunswick antiques store, the sheepskin is from Buckwheat Blossom Farm in Wiscasset, and the chaise was found at a nearby yard sale— surprisingly enough, "it came from an embassy office in Washington, DC," Julie says.

2

3 Minimal background

The textural, bone-colored walls are done in plaster mixed with a bit of titanium white.

4 One-room living

"We moved our bed downstairs to give the boys space to play and sleep on their own," says Julie. "It's an incredible place to wake up. The light at six a.m. is indescribable, and we would have missed it if we had stayed put upstairs." The linens are from Dazed but Amazed.

5 Branch as banister
A long limb from a fallen poplar tree serves as a stair rail.

6 Local lumber
Anthony sourced eastern white cedar for the interiors; the door and window jambs are Douglas fir.

7 New uses for old things
"The hutch is an old pie-cooling cabinet from a local antiques store," Julie says. "We keep the children's clothes in it."

8 Efficient warmth
The woodstove heats the house,
thanks to a clever convection
system: Heated air rises from
the sunken kitchen to the boys'
bedroom above, then drops back
down through a floor vent, where
it's cycled through again.

9 Loom divider
A loom, strung up beside cedar
shelving, is made from hardware-
store supplies and goods from
Spruce Tree Studio, Julie's mother's
shop in Tenants Harbor (see page
211). "We all like to work together
on things, so it feels fun to have an
ongoing project that happens in little
lulls of time and doesn't need to be
put away," Julie says.

10 Undercounter storage
Built-in niches below the sink keep
firewood within easy reach.

11 Mini root cellar
A nook beneath the floor of the
main room offers a cool, dry space
for a larder.

9

10

11

12 Kitchen cupboard
An antique secretary found at
Trillium Soaps (see page 201)
serves as a hutch.

13 Handmade bath
The small washroom features a
poured-in-place concrete bathtub
made by Anthony.

THE MAKERS' HOUSE

14

14 Ad hoc closet
Upstairs, copper pipes are suspended
from the eaves with rope for a
deconstructed, DIY clothes rack.

15 Open concept
High ceilings and generous windows
keep the space from feeling closed in.

16

16 Scrap sauna
Anthony built the small sauna from spare bits and pieces: an existing timber frame, made from remnants of an early-nineteenth-century home and left behind by the land's previous owner, and wood, shingles, and cedar remnants from building the other houses in the clearing. "Even the stove came from a nineteenth-century Finnish log cabin I dismantled," he says.

17 Hydration station
Essential supplies include vintage lanterns and a Walter filter system for fresh water.

18 Eco details
The sauna is faced in burned wood boards, while the Soot House's Colonial-style clapboards are finished with another Japanese technique: fermented paint Anthony made from soot, water, and persimmon. "As the soot paint wears off over time, the runoff will trickle into the soil and be a gentle fertilizer," Julie says. "It's important for us to not just live in nature but with nature, and make sure it is benefiting from us even just a fraction of how much we are benefiting from it."

How to Tap Maples for Syrup

SIKWANI DANA GREW UP MAPLE SYRUPING ON HER PARENTS' FARM AT WINTER'S END, A TRADITION THAT'S BEEN PASSED DOWN THROUGH GENERATIONS. "OUR PEOPLE, THE WABANAKI, HAVE BEEN MAKING MAPLE SYRUP FOR THOUSANDS OF YEARS," SHE SAYS. "THE SAP WOULD HAVE BEEN COLLECTED IN BIRCH BARK BASKETS." SIKWANI AND HER HUSBAND, **NATHAN DANA**, SHARE GLIMPSES OF THEIR LIFE IN SOLON ON TIKTOK AND INSTAGRAM VIA @THE_DANA_HOMESTEAD; HERE, SHE SHARES SIX STEPS FOR TAPPING MAPLES AT HOME.

1 Find the right time. "The maple sugaring season changes slightly every year. The time for syruping is when temperatures are freezing at night and in the low forties with minimal wind during the day."

2 Choose a tree. "Sugar maples tend to have higher sugar content, but red maples can be tapped, too."

3 Gather materials. "Fancy equipment is not necessary, but there are some essentials: a drill, a spout (the drill bit should match the size of the spout), something to collect the sap, and a large pot to boil the sap in."

4 Insert the spout. "There's no need to drill too deep into the tree. The sap flows close to the bark; a couple of inches should keep the spout in the tree." Hang your bucket just below and wait for the sap to run.

5 Boil down the sap. "The key to making the best-tasting maple syrup is cooking the sap outside over a wood fire," though it can be done inside. "You can literally call it good whenever you're happy with the taste and thickness."

6 Prepare for next year. "There's no need to plug the hole when the season is done. Trees are great compartmentalizers and will seal off the wound."

Eliot

THE FLOWER FARMERS' HOUSE

A COUPLE BROUGHT A
CENTURIES-OLD FARMHOUSE
BACK TO ITS BEGINNINGS—WITH
HORSEHAIR PLASTER WALLS,
NAMES ETCHED IN THE BEAMS,
AND SIX-OVER-SIX WINDOWS
THAT LET IN WINTER LIGHT.

Before Bess Piergrossi lived in her Eliot home, she worked as a farmhand at the dairy next door. "I used to dream about living in 'that house over there,'" she says, "never thinking it was in the cards." One day, the farmer she worked for mentioned that the old house might be going on the market. Bess walked over after her shift, knocked on the door, and introduced herself, and she and her husband, Michael Piergrossi, a farmer and former chef, put in an offer that weekend. "The fact that I get to live here is serendipitous and an honor," Bess says. "It's something I think about every day."

As part of the couple's "stewardship" of the place, as they see it, Bess has traced the history of the home through the Eliot Historical Society. "The house was built in 1740 and was the Emery-Frost farm. There is a graveyard in our front yard with several of the Frost and Emery family members," she says—distant relatives of Robert Frost. "Our living room door also has the name 'Olive' etched into it in a child's handwriting."

The farmhouse didn't have plumbing or running water until the 1980s; now "all the plumbing is exposed, running along the walls and ceilings so as not to disturb the horsehair plaster walls. It's beautiful copper, and I love that it's visible," says Bess. She and Michael renovated all the interiors themselves, embracing the undone look and taking away more than they added. "We hand-scraped all the wood floors of several layers of paint, sanded them, removed wallpaper, replastered the walls. Our goal was to strip the house back to its original bones, to how it would have looked as a 'new build' back in 1740." The result? Quiet, poetic interiors where winter light illuminates the excavated walls.

Outside, on their parcel of two and a half acres, the couple runs Hitchfoot Farm, through which they sell flowers, vegetables, and freshly laid eggs at a stand at the end of their drive from April until the first snow. In winter, the couple carries out small old-fashioned tasks: lighting the woodstove and living room fireplace (the main heat sources for the house), and slipping a soapstone slab, warm from the hearth, beneath the covers before getting into bed at night. "This is one of the oldest homes in Maine," says Bess. "Our interaction with it has been a blip in its history, and we imagine it will stand for far longer than we are here. We just want to honor it while we can."

1 Farm kitchen
The couple left the existing dark leathered granite counters intact and stripped the cabinets down to the wood. Pots and pans hang from the original hand-hewn beams.

2 Open pantry
Ceramics and woven baskets, dry goods, a few well-loved cookbooks, and newly collected eggs are displayed on simple shelves.

3 Done/undone
The couple stripped the floors of the decades' layers. "When we started, we had bitten off more than we could chew, but we quickly fell in love with the unfinished look," says Bess.

4 Utility made visible
Exposed copper piping adds to the excavated style.

5 Distressed charm
After wallpaper was removed, some walls were left bare, to timeworn effect.

6 Rustic gatherings
A slender table and an assortment
of seating draped with sheepskins
create an unfussy dining area and
make use of the long, narrow space.

7 Old-school find
A vintage chalkboard—a local
antiques store discovery—hangs
above a nonworking fireplace.

8 Literary object
In the living room, a 14-inch-thick dictionary—an antique find of Bess's—becomes a sculptural curio.

9 Snug space
"Since the beams are low, we removed the baseboards in the living room to make the ceilings seem higher and make the space feel more rustic and less refined," says Bess.

10 Irons in the fire
Two farmhouse musts: a good set of fireplace tools and a sturdy log holder.

11

12

13

14

11 Pattern play
Rosy-hued wallpaper—one of the few finishes the couple hasn't stripped back—makes a sweet backdrop for a bath.

12 Repurposed storage
In true old-house form, there's only one closet in the whole place. Here, a bookshelf finds new purpose as a clothes closet.

13 Neutral texture
Upstairs, a bedroom is left quiet, with layers of white blankets, a vintage sconce, and plaster walls. "I took a Jersey Ice Cream Co. plaster workshop and gave our bedroom a test run," Bess says.

14 DIY bed warmer
The couple heats soapstone slabs by the woodstove and tucks them under the covers before bed.

15

15 Bath bough

A sweep of evergreen, suspended above a bathtub, was inspired by a childhood memory of making wall hangings from foraged finds. "I took the idea and elevated it a bit, with greens gathered from the woods behind our home," says Bess. From the claw-foot tub, she says, "the view is so incredibly relaxing. I had candles wired to the branches in early winter, which made it even more surreal."

16 Sink-side charm

An appealingly old-fashioned way to hang a hand towel: above the sink, with vintage clothespins (Bess found hers at a flea market, ten dollars for a box). The mirrored sconces came with the house.

16

17 Old land

"The landscape has several large flower beds that were here when we bought the home, and new ones that we've created," says Bess. "But most of the landscape is farm pasture, with the cow field in the backyard and the Emery-Frost family graveyard in the front. We also border a large plot of land owned by the land trust, which is used for farming and for recreational walking trails."

How to Start a Mending Practice

JULIE O'ROURKE IS THE FOUNDER OF PLANT-DYED CLOTHING COMPANY RUDY JUDE, AND EVEN AT HOME, SHE'S ALWAYS MAKING: WEAVING RUGS, SEWING QUILTS INTO CLEVER KIDS' CLOTHES, AND REPAIRING TABLECLOTHS BY HAND, AS DOCUMENTED ON HER EVER-POPULAR INSTAGRAM, @RUDYJUDE (AND IN THIS BOOK—SEE PAGE 159). VISIBLE FIXES, WITH JULIE'S APPROACH, ADD CHARM—AND EXTEND THE LIFE OF LINENS. WHETHER YOU'RE PATCHING, STITCHING, OR DARNING, HERE ARE HER SIX TIPS FOR TAKING UP A MENDING PRACTICE OF YOUR OWN.

1 Tackle one piece at a time. Don't accumulate a pile of things to repair; it's easy to get snowed under. "Mend things when they need it," says Julie. "If you find a hole in your tablecloth, fix it in that moment. A small repair could take less than fifteen minutes."

2 Repurpose. "I find the most charm in repairs that are done with things you already have on hand: a patch made with worn-out napkins or stitched with embroidery thread from another project. The randomness is so lovely in a visible mend."

3 Work ahead. Being proactive pays off. "Repair a tiny hole before it turns into a big hole, because it will," says Julie.

4 Fix in found moments. "Bring your mending in the car, sit in the sun or in the corner of your house with it while everyone runs around you."

5 Patience, not perfection. Mending is a process. "Take your time; make slow, purposeful stitches," says Julie. "Don't strive for perfection. Know that the mend will probably tear again sometime, and be ready to fix it over and over again."

6 Pass it on. "Teach someone else how to fix something. Sew on a button with your kid; show a neighbor how to patch something. It's incredible knowledge to be able to share."

Driftwood Hook

Worn smooth and weathered, driftwood from the Maine coast has inspired many a would-be carver—including Remodelista editor Justine Hand and her family, who have been making these hand-carved hooks in their Maine cabin for generations. There, on a tiny island, there's no electricity, no running water—just lots of driftwood, and plenty of time for whittling. The results are the perfect rustic complement to any room.

Driftwood Hook

MATERIALS

Y- OR V-SHAPED DRIFTWOOD
OR FOUND BRANCH, BARK
REMOVED

SAW

WHITTLING KNIFE

VISE

FILE OR PLANE

DRILL

SANDPAPER

2 NAILS OR SCREWS

1 Wood carving is an intuitive exercise in which the final shape of the object is dictated by the branch's form, so pick a piece that appeals to you. Look for a sturdy branch with one or two offshoots that meet the main limb at an approximately 45-degree angle.

2 Determine the desired length of your final piece and saw off the excess on both the main branch and the limb(s) that will form the hook.

3 Then, with your sharpest whittling knife, shave away from yourself to round and taper the edges.

4 Once your shape is honed, secure the branch in a vise and use a file or plane to create a flat surface on the back.

5 Drill a hole on each end of the branch. Make sure your top hole is above the tip of the hook, or you will have difficulty screwing or nailing the hook to the wall.

6 Finally, remove the branch from the vise and smooth it with sandpaper. Hang with nails or screws, as desired.

1

2

3

4

5

6

Balsam Fir Pillow

Balsam fir is the fragrance of Maine. That's why sachets filled with the trees' aromatic needles can be found in every souvenir shop throughout the state. For our reimagined version, we eschewed the expected lobster, lighthouse, and blueberry motifs and instead chose fabrics that reflect the textures and hues of Maine's woodlands and shores.

Balsam Fir Pillow

MATERIALS

BALSAM FIR, EITHER DRIED OR
FRESHLY HARVESTED

CLIPPERS (IF USING FRESH
BALSAM)

FABRIC

SCISSORS

RULER

PEN

SEWING PINS

SEWING MACHINE
(OPTIONAL)

NEEDLE AND THREAD

WIDEMOUTHED FUNNEL
(OPTIONAL)

1 Bulk dried balsam is readily available online. If you wish to harvest your own—say, after clearing a path or taking down the Christmas tree—first you need to learn to distinguish balsam from its fellow conifer, spruce. Balsam has flat needles that are round at the end; spruce needles are square-shaped and have sharp, pointy tips. To prep balsam for your pillow, snip the finer branches into small bits with clippers.

2 Cotton, linen, and wool are the textures of Maine. For a fresh, cool version for summertime, use linen or cotton; if you want to make your pillow cozier, use wool (we repurposed an old wool baby blanket for one of our pillows).

3 Cut two pieces of fabric that are identical in size. Place what will become the outer sides together, mark the outline of your pillow (the size is up to you) with a ruler and pen on what will become the inside, and pin.

4 Sew with a machine or by hand, leaving a 2-inch opening on one side for the balsam. Turn the pillow right side out. Using a widemouthed funnel or your hands, fill the pillow. If using fresh balsam, stuff your pillow very full, as the balsam will compact as it dries. Sew the remaining opening by hand.

NOTE: This project can be scaled down to make sachets, perfect for sock drawers and linen closets, or up to make more generously sized pillows to toss on a bed.

1

2

3

4

Where to Go in Cold Weather

There are many good reasons to head to Maine after Labor Day, in the "off season" when summer vacationers go home and the state feels a little quieter: leaf peeping and apple picking in autumn; skiing, snowshoeing, even dogsledding and ice fishing in winter. Here's our roundup of design-worthy places to visit, organized from south to north. For more on these destinations, see Resources, beginning on page 210.

COREY DANIELS GALLERY
← *Wells*

Owner Corey Daniels curates works by Maine artists as well as found objects in this nationally known gallery in a nineteenth-century Colonial house and connected barn. It's an outlier among the seafood restaurants and flea markets on Route One, and well worth a stop on a drive along the coast.

OLD HOUSE PARTS COMPANY
Kennebunk

You could spend an entire day in this rambling 1872 freight warehouse turned architectural salvage shop and still not see everything. Browse the rooms full of antique mantels, paned windows, glass doorknobs, claw-foot tubs, latches, lighting, vintage soap holders, and other rescues.

PALACE DINER
→ *Biddeford*

Tucked into the rejuvenated mill town of Biddeford, this is Maine's oldest diner, housed in an original 1927 Pollard Company car, one of only two left in the world. It's consistently named one of the country's best restaurants (and draws crowds accordingly). Palace Diner has only fifteen seats and doesn't accept reservations, so arrive early and duck into Rabelais (see the next entry) while you're waiting.

RABELAIS
Biddeford

Bibliophiles and epicures head to Rabelais for a trove of rare and out-of-print cookbooks—one of the largest such collections in the US—plus vintage menus; tomes on horticulture, spirits, table etiquette, and more; even original letters from the likes of Julia Child.

JACKRABBIT AND ELDA
Biddeford

At this pair of restaurants, you feel as if you're in Stockholm, not a former mill building in Maine. The design (pale wood, darkly dramatic wallpaper) is as worth a visit as the Scandinavian-style pastries (Jackrabbit) and elevated tasting menu (Elda).

GOGO REFILL
South Portland

We like this package-free shop for all sorts of earth-friendly household essentials, from dish brushes to wooden combs to reusable produce bags. Or bring your own container and fill up on laundry detergent or castile soap.

SEAWEED CO.
South Portland and Portland

Some of the best-looking dispensaries we've seen are in Maine, where cannabis is a rapidly expanding industry. Stop into these open, clean-lined spaces designed by Caleb Johnson Studio with minimalist smoking accoutrements artfully displayed.

PORTLAND FLEA-FOR-ALL
Portland

This shop in Portland's Arts District is like a flea market with little digging required. Flea-for-All carries an eccentric, ever-rotating stock of antique finds; we particularly like their selection of mid-century-style furniture.

JUDITH
↓ *Portland*

Brooke Beaney's well-appointed shop stocks curated housewares (Saipua soaps, cast-bronze oyster bottle openers by Hawaii-based Mau-House), jewelry by Kate Jones of Maine-based Ursa Major (see page 213), plus some of our favorite clothing brands in sculptural surrounds.

TANDEM COFFEE + BAKERY
↑ *Portland*

The Congress Street outpost of this Portland favorite is housed in a former service station, retrofitted into a bright bakery—and churns out some of the best pastries in town. Look for the BRAKES & SHOCKS sign above the entryway.

PORTLAND FREEDOM TRAIL
Portland

This self-guided tour takes you to addresses important to Black history in Portland, including the site of the Quaker meetinghouse where the antislavery movement in Maine took hold. The highlight is the soaring Abyssinian Meeting House; once the center point of Maine's Underground Railroad and a gathering place for the Black community, it is now protected on the National Register of Historic Places.

SEGUIN TREE DWELLINGS
→ *Georgetown*

The Maine breezes can't be beat in summer, but there's a certain coziness to sleeping high among the pines in these tree house-like cottages in the colder months. Each has its own wood-fired cedar hot tub; one has a Scandinavian woodstove; all are excellent spots for stargazing.

SQUIRE TARBOX INN
↓ *Westport Island*

Longtime friends (and Texan transplants) Lisa Dalton and Michelle Adams transformed an old inn (the original part dates to 1763) on the National Register of Historic Places from "ye olde Colonial style" to clean lined but snug, all while preserving the building's bones. The inn is open with limited availability in the winter months, adding to its quiet appeal.

SAMUEL SNIDER ANTIQUES
Wiscasset

Designer Samuel Snider stitches effortlessly sophisticated garments from one-of-a-kind antique French linens, and now he has a vintage shop of his own (open by appointment in the off-season), stocking eighteenth- and nineteenth-century painted furniture, Early American textiles, and folk art.

THE KINGFISHER & THE QUEEN
Damariscotta

Dip into this shop for small finds—Swedish dishcloths, taper candles—and one-of-a-kind vintage ephemera, curated by a husband-and-wife team.

OLSON HOUSE
Cushing

This farmhouse may look familiar: Glimpsed from below across the rolling lawn, it's almost exactly the framing of Andrew Wyeth's pastoral *Christina's World*. He painted Olson House again and again and once said, "I'd always seem to gravitate back to the house. . . . It was Maine." The house, with its sunny yellow kitchen, woodstove, and wide-plank floors, is now maintained by the Farnsworth Art Museum in Rockland.

TRILLIUM SOAPS
Rockland

In addition to their soaps made with locally collected rainwater (see page 206) and other natural bath essentials, this Rockland shop stocks heirloom linens, vintage flatware, and antiques (like the charming woven stool on page 132).

DAUGHTERS
Rockland

Owner Ariel Birke carries elevated finds for the home—Japanese towels and sculptural washi-wick candles, pieces by ANK Ceramics (see page 204)—as well as consciously made clothing in her thoughtfully designed, minimalist space. We suggest stopping by in autumn; the store is also open by appointment February through April.

MÉ LON TOGO
Searsport and Camden

Drummer and chef Jordan Benissan moved from Togo to Maine to teach music at Colby College, and he opened the first iteration of his West African restaurant in a brightly painted Colonial tavern in Searsport to great acclaim. The 1800s interiors feature Togo-meets-New England spirit with warm terra-cotta-hued walls, ladder-back chairs, and traditional baskets.

LONG GRAIN
Camden

Husband-and-wife team Ravin "Bas" Nakjaroen and Paula Palakawong serve award-winning, locally sourced variations on Asian home cooking and street food on mix-and-match dishes in their Camden restaurant, with vintage kitchen tools as eclectic wall decor.

Balsam fir

The Maine 30

The Maine houses we admire are outfitted both pragmatically and artfully, with utilitarian New England standbys, handmade wares, and accumulated finds that become permanent fixtures (wonderfully mix-and-match mugs in the cottage kitchen, for example). From woven baskets to L.L. Bean boots, here are our all-time favorite Maine classics.

Indoor Wares

Unfussy, effortless, Maine-inspired interiors start with designed-to-last workhorses and thoughtfully handcrafted objects. Here are a few Remodelista favorites—no lobster-themed tchotchkes included. (For more sources and makers, see page 212.)

3 SHAKER-STYLE SEAT
stimberlake.com

Practical, pared-back Shaker furniture is evident in many a Maine home, and these woven-tape chairs and stools can be used as seating or, in a pinch, nightstands. Find traditional options from Timberlake Shaker Furniture or seek out modern iterations by small-batch artisans.

1 ALL-WEATHER COTTON BLANKET
evangelinelinens.com

Simple, all-purpose cotton bedding is warm in winter, cool in summer, and easily washed. Our favorite versions are subtle herringbone and pinstriped throws from Portland-based Evangeline Linens, woven in Maine and reminiscent of a seaside cottage.

2 OLD-SCHOOL TAPER CANDLES
danicacandles.com

A stash of candles is essential, for dinner parties and power outages alike. Danica Design tapers are hand-dipped with precision on the Midcoast using old-world Danish techniques; they're available in a wide range of hues and heights.

4 CERAMIC SERVEWARE
ankceramics.com

Pitchers, plates, and cups by a coterie of Maine ceramicists are equal parts artful and practical. We particularly like the sculptural, one-of-a-kind forms by Camden-based Ariela Nomi Kuh of ANK Ceramics for a statement on the mantel or table.

5 LOCALLY RAISED WOOL
starcroftfiber.com

Some places in Maine look like Ireland, the rambling, rocky land dotted with sheep. And, as on the Emerald Isle, the wet and cold climate means temperature-regulating, moisture-wicking wool is a must. There's no shortage of local, natural-hued wool yarn to be found, but we particularly like the offerings from Starcroft Wool & Yarn, which uses wool made from sheep raised on three uninhabited islands.

7 TRADITIONAL WINDSOR CHAIR
windsorchair.com

Though Windsor chairs originated in Old England, there's something about them that feels quintessential New England–and, with a spindle back and saddle seat, they're both stately and comfortable. The most well-known local versions are made by Windsor Chairmakers in Lincolnville.

9 IRON STORAGE HOOKS
blackdogironworks.com

A hand-forged iron hook is ideal for hanging jackets and dog leashes in the entry or corralling wet towels on the way in from the beach. We prefer plain and pared-back over ornamental: The beauty is in the simplicity.

10 WOVEN WABANAKI BASKET
abbemuseum.org

Basketmaking–using sweetgrass, bark, and black ash wood to sometimes ornate effect–has been part of Wabanaki culture for centuries in the land now known as Maine. Now, even as black ash trees are in danger from the arrival of the destructive emerald ash borer, a new generation of Indigenous makers is carrying on the age-old tradition. Find a variety of baskets, like the one pictured, by Micmac artist Rose Anne Bernard, via the Abbe Museum (see page 123).

6 SHAKER FLAT BROOM
maineshakers.com

A well-made broom keeps floors neat and tidy and looks good on display, too. It was the Shakers who discovered that binding brooms flat created an ideal cleaning tool, and Sabbathday Lake Shaker Village (see page 121) offers an array of options by Maine-born broomsquire Everett Bailey. (Hang, never stand, brooms to make the bristles last longer.)

8 FOLDING CAMP COT
byerofmaine.com

We're longtime fans of Byer of Maine's versatile camp furniture, designed for the outdoors but equally at home inside. Their wood-framed Maine Heritage cot works great as an ad hoc sofa or pop-up guest bed.

11 HARD-WEARING BOAT PAINT
epifanes.com

Glossy, indestructible boat paint is a staple finish for lobster shacks, boat decks, and guesthouse floors alike—any place that gets lots of traffic and could benefit from a little water resistance (think tracked-in mud and melting snow). Marine finishes company Epifanes began in 1902 in the Netherlands and continues to offer boat paints and enamels via their US base in Thomaston, Maine.

12 ECO-CONSCIOUS KITCHEN LINENS
amphitritestudio.com

We seek out reusable, eco-friendly cloth napkins and towels over disposable paper goods, always. A wide array of Maine makers sew, weave, and print kitchen linens using natural fibers and dyes, like Amphitrite Studio's classically striped tea towels, sewn on the coast.

13 CARRYALL CANVAS TOTES
llbean.com

The L.L. Bean canvas bag is an icon for a reason: Crafted in Maine since 1944 and available in a multitude of colorways, it's durable enough to corral shoes in an entryway, store spare blankets, or tote essentials to the beach.

14 BOTANICAL SOAPS
trilliumsoaps.com

Forget perfumy gift-shop versions; our favorite Maine-made soaps are eco-friendly and subtly scented. Rockland-based Trillium Soaps crafts small-batch bars using natural ingredients like Maine seaweed, pine, and rainwater collected down the street from the workshop.

15 FARMERS' ALMANAC
store.farmersalmanac.com

No matter where you live, the Maine-published *Farmers' Almanac* (not to be confused with *The Old Farmer's Almanac*, published in New Hampshire) is a handy book to have around for smart household tidbits and old-school know-how, from which healing herbs to add to a bath to ideal seed-starting dates and DIY cleaning potions.

16 IRON FIREPLACE TOOLS
wicksforge.com

In the spirit of long-lasting, well-made tools, we like forged fireplace tools made by blacksmiths the state over. Seek out something custom from the likes of Wicks Forge, or search for "fireplace tools" on Etsy (and set the location filter to "Maine").

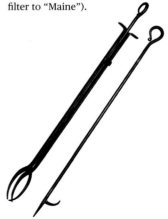

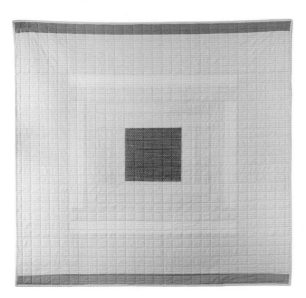

17 HERITAGE QUILTS
smithsgeneral.com

Handmade quilts have a long history in Maine and they're enjoying a revival. Find a vintage quilt via flea markets and eBay; we're also partial to Smith's General in Yarmouth, which offers minimal, modern versions.

18 HAND-CARVED WOODEN SPOONS
hellotreeline.com

There's no shortage of excellent woodwork in Maine, and a rustic, organic spoon is a small example of this craft that every kitchen can accommodate. Look for wooden implements (and bowls) by Monika Pfistner of Treeline, carved in western Maine.

19 PAINE'S LOG-CABIN INCENSE BURNER
paineproducts.com

These tiny log-cabin incense burners have been produced by Paine's for decades. Add natural incense (made in Auburn, from balsam branches) to the center of the log cabin, light, and close the lid for a curl of smoke from the chimney—a welcome sight (and smell) during a Maine winter.

20 WOVEN POTATO BASKET
See Resources, page 212

The potato basket is a Wabanaki creation, designed when Aroostook County's famous potato harvest was done by hand. Use one to hold kitchen linens, tote a picnic, or collect berries; check out the offerings from basketmaker Richard Silliboy, whose family's sturdy, precisely made potato baskets have been prized for decades, or find a hard-to-come-by vintage version via eBay.

21 L.L. BEAN BOOTS
llbean.com

A pair of these trusty boots can be found beside every front door in Maine—so much so that they've become a sort of state icon. The design has been virtually unchanged since 1911, when Leon Leonwood Bean made the first pairs in his brother's basement, specially designed—with leather uppers and rubber soles—to keep feet dry in the Maine outdoors.

Outdoor Wares

Mainers know how to outfit themselves—and their houses—for the salt air, wind, and strong sun that can define a year Down East. For the front porch, outdoor shower, and beyond, here are some rugged, time-tested local products for outdoor living. (For more sources and makers, see page 212.)

22 WEATHERPROOF CEDAR SHINGLES
dowseasternwhiteshingles.com

The humble cedar shingle is a centuries-old staple of Maine exteriors, particularly on the coast. Laid tightly together as siding, the shingles are weatherproof, highly insulating, and long-lasting, and when left untreated, they age gracefully to gray. Some family-owned operations, like Dow's, still make shingles and old-fashioned hand-split shakes.

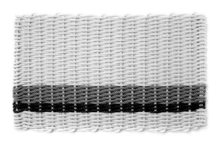

24 NAUTICAL ROPE DOORMAT
theropeco.com

The repurposed-rope doormat, made from mold- and mildew-resistant lobstering rope and easily hosed down, is as indestructible as it is charming. The Rope Co. in Tenants Harbor makes hardy (and cheerfully color-blocked) options.

25 BILL MOSS TENT
ebay.com

"A tent to me is a piece of sculpture you can get into," the fabric artist Bill Moss once said. In the 1950s, Moss created the portable Pop-Tent, which revolutionized camping as we know it, and went on to open Moss Tent Works in Camden, Maine, where he created clean-lined, architectural tents and canopies. His timeless, durable designs are still available on eBay—finding one is the outdoor equivalent of scoring an original Eames chair.

23 WIRE CLAMMING BASKET
maineclamgear.com

These coated-wire baskets were designed to hold fresh-caught clams but work rather well to corral soaps and shampoos in the outdoor shower, too. Maine Clam Gear Co. sells real-deal, no-fuss versions.

27 WOOD OARS AND PADDLES
shawandtenney.com

"We don't cut corners, because as any seasoned Maine guide would tell you, when you take shortcuts, you get lost." This is the motto of sorts of Shaw & Tenney, Orono-based makers of fine wood oars and paddles. Turned on the same lathe since 1858, their wares are designed for water exploration but beautiful enough to display.

26 CLASSIC CANOE
oldtowncanoe.com

Originally used by the Wabanaki, the canoe has come to symbolize Maine's spirit of exploration and the outdoors. The largest maker of canoes in the US is Old Town, based in Old Town, Maine.

28 TRUSTY AXE
bnctools.com

Every Mainer knows the value of a well-made and easy-to-use axe, like one from Brant & Cochran in South Portland, for splitting small logs and kindling.

29 HANDPICKED NATIVE SEEDS
shop.wildseedproject.net

The mission of Wild Seed Project is to preserve Maine's native flowers, trees, and grasses. They offer a wide catalog of seeds–bluets, bunchberry, wild strawberry, meadowsweet, and more–all collected from private gardens across the state.

30 ORIGINAL MAINE FLAG
maineflagcompany.com

Mainers have recently repopularized the more minimal state flag design used from 1901 to 1909, and in every town, you'll see the flag flying proudly from stoops and storefronts. We like those made by Maine Flag Company, cut and stitched in the state.

Places to Go

FARMS AND FLOWER STANDS

Smithereen Farm
767 Leighton Point Road
Pembroke
smithereenfarm.com

Snug Harbor Farm
87 Western Avenue
Kennebunk
snugharborfarm.com

Turner Farm
73 Turner Farm Road
North Haven
turner-farm.com

LODGINGS

Aragosta at Goose Cove
300 Goose Cove Road
Deer Isle
aragostamaine.com

The Brooklin Inn
22 Reach Road
Brooklin
thebrooklininn.com

Lincolnville Motel
4 Sea View Drive
Lincolnville
lincolnvillemotel.com

Nebo Lodge
11 Mullins Lane
North Haven
nebolodge.com

Seguin Tree Dwellings
Georgetown
seguinmaine.com

Seven Lakes Inn
168 Main Street
Belgrade
sevenlakesinn.com

Squire Tarbox Inn
1181 Main Road
Westport Island
squiretarboxinn.com

Terramor Outdoor Resort
1453 ME-102
Bar Harbor
terramoroutdoorresort.com

Tops'l Farm
365 Bremen Road
Waldoboro
topslfarm.com

MUSEUMS, CULTURAL INSTITUTIONS, AND POINTS OF INTEREST

Abbe Museum
26 Mount Desert Street
Bar Harbor
abbemuseum.org

Abyssinian Meeting House
75 Newbury Street
Portland

Center for Maine Contemporary Art
21 Winter Street
Rockland
cmcanow.org

Farnsworth Art Museum
16 Museum Street
Rockland
farnsworthmuseum.org

Tours of the Olson House, the subject of Andrew Wyeth's *Christina's World*, can be arranged through the museum.

Good Life Center
372 Harborside Road
Harborside
goodlife.org

Haystack Mountain School of Crafts
89 Haystack School Drive
Deer Isle
haystack-mtn.org

Maine Historical Society
489 Congress Street
Portland
mainehistory.org

A guide to the Portland Freedom Trail, with stops at Black history sites throughout the city, is available via the Maine Historical Society's website.

New Sweden Historical Society
116 Station Road
New Sweden
facebook.com/ NewSwedenHistoricalSociety

Portland Museum of Art and Winslow Homer Studio
7 Congress Square
Portland
portlandmuseum.org

The museum also offers visits to the Winslow Homer Studio on Prouts Neck, where the painter lived and worked from 1883 to 1910, via guided tour.

Sabbathday Lake Shaker Village
707 Shaker Road
New Gloucester
maineshakers.com

Washington Baths
145 Washington Avenue
Portland
washingtonbaths.com

RESTAURANTS AND BAKERIES

Chase's Daily
96 Main Street
Belfast
chasesdaily.me

Elda
14 Main Street, 2nd Floor
Biddeford
eldamaine.com

Jackrabbit
14 Main Street, First Floor
Biddeford
jackrabbitmaine.com

Long Grain
20 Washington Street
Camden
longgraincamden.com

The Lost Kitchen
22 Mill Street
Freedom
findthelostkitchen.com

Mé Lon Togo
10 Leland Street
Rockland

375 E Main Street
Searsport
melontogorestaurant.com

Palace Diner
18 Franklin Street
Biddeford
palacedinerme.com

Tandem Coffee + Bakery
742 Congress Street
Portland
tandemcoffee.com

SHOPS, GALLERIES,
AND ANTIQUES STORES

Blanche + Mimi
184 Middle Street
Portland
blancheandmimi.com

Corey Daniels Gallery
2208 Post Road
Wells
coreydanielsgallery.com

Daughters
442 Main Street
Rockland
shopdaughters.me

GoGo Refill
64 East Street
South Portland
gogorefill.com

Hopkins Wharf Gallery
7 Hopkins Wharf
North Haven
hopkinswharfgallery.com

Judith
131 Middle Street
Portland
shopjudith.com

The Kingfisher & the Queen
79 Main Street
Damariscotta
thekingfisherandthequeen.com

Marlinespike Chandlery
58 West Main Street
Stonington
marlinespike.com

Marston House
18 Main Street
Vinalhaven
marstonhouse.com

Marston House Wiscasset
101 Main Street
Wiscasset
marstonhousewiscasset.com

North Haven Gift Shop
26 Main Street
North Haven
northhavengiftshop.com

Old House Parts Company
1 Trackside Drive
Kennebunk
oldhouseparts.com

Portia's Barn
portiaclark.com

Portland Architectural Salvage
131 Preble Street
Portland
portlandsalvage.com

Portland Flea-for-All
585 Congress Street
Portland
portlandfleaforall.com

The Post Supply
65 Washington Avenue
Portland
thepostsupply.com

Rabelais
2 Main Street, Suite 18-214
Biddeford
rabelaisbooks.com

Samuel Snider Antiques
54 Water Street
Wiscasset
samuelsnider.wordpress.com

SeaWeed Co.
185 Running Hill Road
South Portland

23 Marginal Way, Suite 7
Portland

seaweedmaine.com

Spruce Tree Studio
68 Main Street
Tenants Harbor
sprucetreestudio.com

Sugar Tools
29 Bay View Street
Camden
sugartoolsshop.com

Trillium Soaps
216 South Main Street
Rockland
trilliumsoaps.com

Artisans and Makers

AXES

Brant & Cochran
bnctools.com

Snow & Nealley
theworkingaxes.com

BASKETS

Gabriel Frey
gabrielfreybaskets.com

Jeremy Frey
jeremyfreybaskets.com

Richard Silliboy
11 Medicine Wheel Road
Littleton

Sarah Sockbeson
sarahsockbeson.com

Stephen Zeh
stephenzeh.com

BLANKETS AND QUILTS

Evangeline Linens
332 Fore Street
Portland
evangelinelinens.com

Maine Woolens
124 Main Street
Freeport
mainewoolens.com

Smith's General
smithsgeneral.com

Swans Island Company
231 Atlantic Highway
Northport

2 Bay View Street
Camden

swansislandcompany.com

BOAT PAINT

Epifanes
epifanes.com

BROOMS

Sabbathday Lake Shaker Village
707 Shaker Road
New Gloucester
maineshakers.com

CANDLES AND FRAGRANCE

Danica Design Candles
569 West Street
Rockport
danicacandles.com

Paine Products
paineproducts.com

CANOES, OARS, AND PADDLES

Northwoods Canoe Co.
wooden-canoes.com

Old Town
oldtowncanoe.com

Shaw & Tenney
20 Water Street
Orono
shawandtenney.com

CANVAS TOTES

L.L. Bean
95 Main Street
Freeport
llbean.com

Port Canvas
39 Limerick Road
Arundel
portcanvas.com

Rogue Industries
650 Cape Road
Standish
rogue-industries.com

Sea Bags
123 Commercial Street
Portland

25 Custom House Wharf
Portland

seabags.com

Studio Crie
studiocrie.com

CERAMICS

ANK Ceramics
46 Elm Street
Camden
ankceramics.com

Ayumi Horie
ayumihorie.com

Campfire Pottery
5 South Street
Portland
campfirepottery.com

Elephant Ceramics
elephantceramics.com

Monohanako
monohanako.com

Softset Ceramics
2 Taylor Street
Portland
softsetceramics.com

DOORMATS

Cape Porpoise Trading Co.
capeporpoisetradingco.com

The Rope Co.
theropeco.com

FURNITURE

American Windsor Chair Company at New England Joinery
641 Route 135
Monmouth
americanwindsorchaircompany.com

Bicyclette
98 Front Street, Unit 402
Bath
bicyclettefurniture.com

Byer of Maine
byerofmaine.com

Chilton Furniture
chiltons.com

Heide Martin Design Studio
10 Farwell Drive
Rockland
heidemartin.com

Huston & Company
hustonandcompany.com

Thos. Moser
149 Main Street
Freeport
thosmoser.com

Timberlake Shaker & Custom Furniture
stimberlake.com

Weather Furniture
131 Washington Avenue
Portland
weatherfurniture.com

Windsor Chairmakers
2596 Atlantic Highway
Lincolnville
windsorchair.com

GARDEN HODS AND CLAMMING BASKETS

Johnny's Selected Seeds
johnnyseeds.com

Maine Clam Gear Co.
736 Leighton Point Road
Pembroke
maineclamgear.com

LEATHERWARES

Bell & Beacon
52 Center Street, Suite 2
Portland
bellandbeacon.com

Loquat
loquatshop.com

33 By Hand
33byhand.com

LINENS AND HOUSEWARES

Always Piper
alwayspiper.com

Amphitrite Studio
amphitritestudio.com

The Cultivated Thread
thecultivatedthread.com

Erin Flett
2 Main Street
Gorham
erinflett.com

Tachee
shoptachee.com

MAINE FLAGS

Maine Flag Company
maineflagcompany.com

Original Maine
20 Hampshire Street
Portland
originalmaine.me

METALWARES

Aaron Beck, Blacksmith
handwroughttools.com

Black Dog Ironworks
blackdogironworks.com

Black Swan Handmade
blackswanhandmade.com

Erica Moody
ericamoody.com

Nick Rossi Knives
nickrossiknives.com

Ursa Major
katejones.us

Wicks Forge
wicksforge.com

Wilson Forge
wilsonforge.com

NATIVE SEEDS

Wild Seed Project
shop.wildseedproject.net

RUGS AND FLOORCLOTHS

Addie Peet
addiepeet.com

Angela Adams Designs
angelaadams.com

SHINGLES AND SIDING

Dow's Eastern White Shingles & Shakes
dowseasternwhiteshingles.com

Longfellow's Cedar Shingles & Shakes
longfellowscedarshingles.com

SOAPS AND SELF-CARE

Island Apothecary
islandapothecary.com

SoulShine Soap Company
soulshinesoapcompany.com

Trillium Soaps
216 South Main Street
Rockland
trilliumsoaps.com

TENTS

Moss Tent Works
billmosstents.com

WOODEN WARES

Carved Wooden Spoons
carvedwoodenspoons.com

Casey's Wood Products
caseyswood.com

Danielle Rose Byrd
daniellerosebyrd.com

Karina K. Steele
karinaksteele.com

Rusted Pulchritude
rustedpulchritude.com

Treeline
hellotreeline.com

WOOL AND YARN

Bartlettyarns
20 Water Street
Harmony
bartlettyarns.com

Lana Plantae
lanaplantae.com

Loohoo Wool Dryer Balls
loo-hoo.com

Seacolors Yarnery
45 Hopkins Road
Washington
getwool.com

Starcroft Wool & Yarn
starcroftfiber.com

Many people contributed their design acumen to this project, including the Remodelista editorial team: Julie Carlson, Margot Guralnick, Fan Winston, and Justine Hand; our publisher, Josh Groves, lent endless logistical support. This book was almost entirely produced and written during the COVID-19 pandemic and would not have been possible without the nimbleness, hard work, and grace of Greta Rybus, our photographer, and Justine Hand, who produced and shot the DIY projects remotely.

Much appreciation goes to Jennifer Wagner, who gave the book shape and a visual spirit through her creative direction. We've long admired the work of artist Lucy Augé, and we are fortunate to include her ephemeral, evocative sketches of Maine flora in these pages.

We owe a huge amount of thanks to the homeowners and architecture studios who appear on these pages: Norelius Studio and the owners of the farmhouse in South Bristol; Maria Berman and Brad Horn of Berman Horn Studio; Donna McNeil; Fiona and Tony Hooper, who worked with architect Sheila Bonnell; David Hopkins and David Wilson; Severine von Tscharner Fleming; Nadja Zerunian and Nick van Praag, who worked with the team at OPAL Architecture; Jocie Dickson of Jocelyn O Dickson Architecture and Graham Dickson; Julie O'Rourke and Anthony Esteves; and Bess and Michael Piergrossi.

We're also grateful to our local experts, who generously provided snapshots of Maine life: Erin French, Molly O'Rourke, Kazeem Lawal, Sharon and Paul Mrozinski, Michelle Provençal, Gardner Waldeier, Hanako Nakazato and Prairie Stuart-Wolff, Sikwani and Nathan Dana, and Julie O'Rourke.

Most important, thanks to the talented team at Artisan, including publisher Lia Ronnen and editor extraordinaire Bridget Monroe Itkin, art director Suet Chong, production editor Sibylle Kazeroid, copy editor Paula Brisco, production director Nancy Murray, and production manager Donna G. Brown.

Lastly, special thanks to two members of the all-woman team at the Lost Kitchen, Ashley Savage and Nancy Buckley; to Bo Bartlett and Betsy Eby, whose Maine still life with lobster opens the book; and to Tracy Weber at Blue Aster Native Plants for her insights on native Maine flora. For their assistance with the DIY projects, we'd like to thank Chris Nagle of Outermost Home, Sheila Bonnell, Marnie Campbell, MMclay, and kePottery.

Notes on Native Flora

From the dried husks of late autumn to the hopeful blooms of spring, here's a closer look at the Maine botanicals representing the seasons in this book.

SPRING COLUMBINE
AQUILEGIA CANADENSIS

With its delicate harlequin blooms of yellow and red dancing at the end of a tall, slender stalk, wild columbine at first glance resembles a woodland sprite. But these otherworldly beauties are real, a gift of the Maine spring.

Despite its dainty appearance, *A. canadensis* is a true rugged Mainer, able to withstand salt air, rocky soil, and shaded woods. It also has a bit of a restless nature: Year after year, it may "travel" around the garden to any open spot. And if you do see a pair of miniature wings among columbine's bright blooms, it is most likely a hummingbird. They, and other pollinators, love these long blossoms.

SUMMER LUPINE
LUPINUS PERENNIS

Almost no flower says Maine like lupine. For several weeks each June, its splendid spires transform Maine's highways and fields into a profusion of purple. It may surprise many to learn, however, that *L. polyphyllus*, the lupine that dominates the summer landscape Down East, is not in fact native to New England.

Sundial or wild lupine (*L. perennis*) is the native variety. It's smaller but no less beautiful than its western cousins, which have taken over to such an extent that native lupine is endangered throughout New England and extinct in the wilds of Maine. More's the pity, since this rare beauty is the only larval host of the endangered Karner blue butterfly.

AUTUMN THISTLE
CIRSIUM SPECIES

If thistles only remind you of Scotland, think again: They thrive in Maine, too. Frequently mistaken for their invasive cousins, beneficial native varieties, such as field or swamp thistles, are often eradicated. But these gentler thistles are an important part of the local ecosystem, feeding both birds and pollinating insects, so it's important to learn to distinguish them. Invasive thistles are quite prickly; native field and swamp thistles have softer stalks.

Native thistles are great for the garden year-round. Their pink to pale purple blooms peak in August; then, long after summer's bounty, their frost-covered husks add an architectural element to the winter garden.

WINTER WINTERBERRY
ILEX VERTICILLATA

As winter descends and visitors have fled south, one Vacationland native is still welcoming tourists: Winterberry, with its vibrant red berries, feeds forty-nine species of bird, many of which migrate from out of state.

For humans, too, winterberry is a hibernal favorite. When earth and water and sky turn the same steely gray or become blanketed in a veil of white, winterberry's vermilion color is a welcome break in the monochrome landscape. Bring a bundle inside as seasonal decor; just be sure to leave some for the birds..

About the Author

Annie P. Quigley is a senior editor at Remodelista; her work has also appeared in the *Wall Street Journal* and *Travel + Leisure*, among other publications. She is a graduate of New York University and lives in Portland, Maine.

About the Contributors

Julie Carlson founded the home design website Remodelista in 2007 with three design-minded friends; Gardenista and the Organized Home soon followed, as well as a series of design books published by Artisan. She is a graduate of Brown University.

Greta Rybus is a photojournalist based in Maine. Originally from Idaho, she documents stories about human connections to the natural world for magazines, newspapers, and other publications.

Justine Hand is a photographer, stylist, and Remodelista contributing editor. Based in Newton, Massachusetts, Hand splits her summers between Cape Cod and Maine.

Jennifer Wagner is a Hudson Valley, New York–based creative director and graphic designer who has worked with Phaidon and *Martha Stewart Living*. She loves travel, food, gardening, and family.

Lucy Augé, who works from her studio in the Bath, England, countryside, is known for capturing fleeting moments of nature's evolution and seasons in her pieces. She is also the founder of art print retailer Atelier Augé, which features work from her archive of botanical illustrations.

Lily Edgerton graduated from Brown University, where she majored in English and Theatre Arts & Performance Studies. In addition to Remodelista, she has worked at McIntosh & Otis and W. W. Norton & Company.

Eleanor McCole is a graduate of Bowdoin College. A Pacific Northwest native, she now lives and works in Brunswick, Maine.

Olivia Nash is a student at Brown University; originally from Rye, New York, she interned with Remodelista in the fall of 2020.